THE HERMITAGE

ALFA - COLOUR

Introduction by *Mikhail Piotrovsky*
Text by *Regina Kogan* and *Tatyana Chukova*
Translation from the Russian by *Paul Williams*
Design by *Oleg Voyevodin* and *Vitaly Suslov*
Computer layout by *Vladimir Krakovsky*
and *Oleg Popov*

ISBN 5-900959-20-1

THE HERMITAGE

ALFA-COLOUR
2005

Fiodor Rokotov. *Portrait of Catherine II.* *Ca.* 1770

The Hermitage and its Traditions

The Hermitage is a truly great museum. It has only a few fellows around the globe, comparable for the scale and quality of the collections, the size and beauty of the exhibition halls, the encyclopaedic display of world culture and art. They are the Louvre, the Metropolitan Museum of Art, and the British Museum together with the National Gallery.

Even in that illustrious group, however, there are certain unique features that set the Hermitage apart. Nowhere else is a museum of culture so tightly fused with history, the brilliant and tragic chronicle of Russia in which it always played an active role. The museum was part of the imperial residence, a single whole comprising Hermitage, Theatre and Winter Palace. From the moment Catherine the Great began placing her collections in a special part of the palace set aside for unofficial receptions and called by the French name *Hermitage*, suggesting a place of solitude, the museum was the scene of many historical events. Today's Hermitage combines in a wondrous manner Scythian gold, Rembrandt paintings, Grecian vases, paintings by Matisse and Picasso with the main Throne Room of the Russian Empire, a gallery of portraits commemorating the victory over Napoleon, Catherine's rooms, the study in which Alexander II died of his wounds, and the Small Dining-Room where the Provisional Government was arrested.

Vasily Sadovnikov. *View of southern facade of the Winter Palace*. **1839. Watercolour**

Konstantin Ukhtomsky. *The St George Hall.* **1862. Watercolour**

The spirit of Russian history wanders the corridors and halls of the Hermitage. This gives the museum a special emotional charge that is felt by every visitor. The Hermitage is a significant phenomenon in Russian culture and Russian history. More than that, it is a symbol of a Russian cultural tradition founded on an openness to the whole world, with no cultural trend regarded as alien. Through both its past and its present, the Hermitage demonstrates that our cultural heritage embraces Scythian art, the Russian icon, Ancient Roman portraits, Rembrandt, the Russian Baroque, the Cubism of Picasso, and the abstraction of Kandinsky. The Hermitage was a major contributor to this aspect of Russian culture, an aspect that surprises many.

The Hermitage is a Russian historical monument, yet it is also a symbol of glorious Russian statehood. The Hermitage is famous for its ability to survive.

It has endured successive evacuations in the course of three wars, the great Winter Palace fire of 1837, and the storming of the palace in 1917.

The Hermitage weathered the period of revolutionary catastrophes, survived despite selling sprees and wholesale redistribution of stocks between museums. It escaped the clutches of Nazi plunderers and continued to be the chief cultural "window on Europe" for Soviet Russia. When Russia remembered about its past, the Hermitage proved ready to reacquaint the country with its national heritage in a dignified, responsible manner through exhibitions and publications.

The Hermitage has always been a museum that looks outwards to the world. To a significant extent it can be said to have been one of the main expressions of the policy of openness towards Europe initiated by Peter the Great. After becoming a public

Konstantin Ukhtomsky. *The Winter Palace. The Malachite Room.* **1865. Watercolour**

Luigi Premazzi. *The Crimson Study.* **1869. Watercolour**

Luigi Premazzi. *The New Hermitage. Tent-Roofed Hall.* **1858. Watercolour**

museum, the Hermitage played an immense educational role, giving those active in Russian culture access to the wider world; and later introducing the ordinary people of Socialist Russia to the fundamentals of world art. The Hermitage has revealed the history of the new Russia to the world. The museum's immense collections, its displays and its educational activities directed towards the most varied sections of the population. Everyone — from schoolchildren to profoundly knowledgeable connoisseurs of art — will find things that interest and appeal to them here.

The Hermitage has always been actively engaged in collecting. The sensational purchases made by Catherine the Great and Alexander II have gone down in history. Remarkable too was the contribution of the Imperial Archaeological Commission. While saving the nation's cultural heritage during the revolution, the museum managed to find itself a proper role in the cultural life of the Soviet Union. In the extremely difficult post-war years the Hermitage's pioneering archaeological researches and discoveries succeeded in maintaining its worldwide reputation and expanding its stocks.

Today the Hermitage is again actively filling its storerooms and its displays. The museum is constantly expanding, seeking to put everything it has on show. Work is currently underway to implement

Eduard Hau. *The New Hermitage. The Large Skylight Hall.* **1853. Watercolour**

a major plan for the general reconstruction of the Hermitage. The Menshikov Palace has been restored to become a new centre of museum life. The Hermitage Theatre has been reconstructed and theatrical activities have become an important element in the Hermitage's existence. The Winter Palace of Peter the Great, discovered during excavations and now restored, has been opened to the public. Restoration of the stateroom interiors and reconstruction of the main exhibitions is continuing. Construction of a special repository, where the famous "reserves" of the Hermitage will be made accessible to researchers and ordinary visitors alike, is drawing to a close. Work is going on to create a fundamentally new Museum of Decorative Art in the General Staff building. The Hermitage has many plans and much work to do.

The museum has repeatedly fulfilled its historical mission and its duty to society. It has something to show and to tell, and tries to do so in such a way as to bring pleasure to people from all over the world and to bring benefit to its own country.

MIKHAIL PIOTROVSKY
Director of the Hermitage
Professor of Historical Sciences
Corresponding Member of the Russian Academy
of Sciences and the Russian Academy of Arts.

The Winter Palace. **Detail of the facade**

THE WINTER PALACE

The Hermitage is the largest museum in Russia, with over 2,800,000 works of art and items of cultural and historical interest in its possession. The items are divided between several collections: painting, graphic art, sculpture, applied art, numismatics and archaeological finds.

The museum is reckoned to have been founded in 1764, the year Catherine II acquired 225 paintings by Western European artists from the Berlin merchant Gotzkowsky. This event marked the beginning of systematic art collecting in Russia.

The Winter Palace.
Architect Francesco Bartolommeo Rastrelli, 1754–62

Catherine's personal apartments included rooms set aside for her collections of jewels, porcelain, cameos and other engraved stones. The French word "hermitage", implying a place to withdraw, a place of solitude, became attached to these rooms. Subsequently the name "Hermitage" became attached to the great museum belonging to the Russian rulers, and later to the state.

Today the exhibition halls and stores of the Hermitage occupy a number of buildings created in the eighteenth and nineteenth centuries by some of the finest architects working in Russia.

The oldest is the Winter Palace, constructed in 1754–62 by Francesco Bartolommeo Rastrelli (1700–1771) for Empress Elizabeth, daughter of Peter the Great. The palace, one of the best works of the Russian

Baroque, became the official residence of the Russian imperial family and remained so until the twentieth century. (The museum exhibits were installed in the palace in the 1920s and 1930s.)

Over the long history of the palace, its outward appearance has changed little, while the look of the interiors — the state rooms and particularly the extensive living quarters — was altered on a number of occasions. In December 1837 there was a major fire in the palace that raged for over thirty hours and destroyed all the decoration inside the building. The imperial residence was restored within fifteen months, by the spring of 1839. The new interiors, however, reflected the tastes of the mid-nineteenth century.

We can get some idea of the original appearance of the palace from the Grand Staircase (also known as the Ambassadors' or Jordan Staircase), recreated after the fire by the architect Vasily Stasov (1769–1848). He adhered closely to the eighteenth-century plans (Nicholas I personally ordered that "the Grand Staircase be restored entirely as it was"). The complex organization of space here, the monumental and exultant quality of the architectural forms, the unfettered decorativeness with an abundance of sculpture and painting, moulding and gilding allow us to appreciate the chief characteristics of Baroque architecture. The white Carrara marble used for the steps and the carved balustrade contrasts strikingly with the smooth polished columns of grey Serdobol (Karelian) granite on the upper landing. The walls, finished in white artificial marble, are adorned with moulded *rocaille* ornament gleaming in the abundant light that pours in through the huge windows and is reflected by the mirrors on the opposite wall. The decoration of the staircase is complemented by numerous allegorical statues; the ceiling is enlivened by a painting depicting Mount Olympus by the Italian painter Gasparo Diziani (1689–1767/68).

The Jordan (Ambassadors') Staircase. **Architect Francesco Bartolommeo Rastrelli, 1754–62**

The Jordan (Ambassadors') Staircase
The upper landing

The Jordan (Ambassadors') Staircase
The lower flight

17

Jean-Marc Nattier. *Portrait of Catherine I.* 1717

Jean-Marc Nattier. *Portrait of Peter I.* 1717

The upper landing of the staircase is the starting-point for the Winter Palace's suites of state rooms that were intended for formal ceremonies and court celebrations. The decoration of these halls reflected not only the tastes of nineteenth-century Russia, but also recent events in the country's history.

The larger suite of rooms opens with the Field Marshals' Hall, created in 1833–34 to the design of the architect Auguste Montferrand (1786–1858) in the traditions of Russian Classicism (the style that succeeded the Baroque in the second half of the eighteenth century). After the 1837 fire, Stasov restored this interior, like the Grand Staircase, almost entirely to its former appearance. In the nineteenth century large formal portraits of Russian field marshals hung in the hall, which determined its name. Artificial marble, a material extensively employed in architecture at the time, was again utilized here. The white walls have a matte finish, while the paired Ionic columns and pilasters have been polished. Equally typical for the Classical era is the use in the Field Marshals' Hall

of *grisaille* painting, where shades of a single colour create the illusion of three-dimensional moulding.

Today the Field Marshals' Hall displays one of the many state coaches belonging to the Hermitage collection — the "great carriage" which is believed to have been made for the coronation of Catherine I, the wife of Peter the Great. The coach also took part in later ceremonies including the coronations of Catherine II, Paul I, Alexander II and Nicholas II. (Russian rulers were crowned in the Assumption Cathedral in Moscow and the coach was conveyed there on a special platform.) This impressive conveyance may have been commissioned from the Gobelins Factory by Peter the Great when he visited Paris in 1717.

The huge body of the coach is decorated with carved woodcarving, cast bronze and embroidered golden velvet. The painted inserts (the noted artist François Boucher may have been involved in the work) depict allegorical figures (Wisdom, Law-Abidingness, Peace, Charity, and others), as well as various characters and attributes with a maritime theme (*putti* riding dolphins, naiads, and so on). The latter were especially popular in early-eighteenth-century Russia as a consequence of the Northern War that gave the country access to the Baltic Sea.

The great carriage was restored in 1990–91. Some fifty specialists from the Hermitage's own restoration workshops took part in the project.

The age of Peter the Great is represented in the museum by works of painting, sculpture, graphic and applied art. The Hermitage can boast some personal possessions of the Emperor and several portraits of him. In 1717, for example, the French artist Jean-Marc Nattier (1685–1766), one of the most fashionable painters of the day, painted a pair of formal portraits of Peter and Catherine. The imperial couple are depicted with the badges and sashes of Russian orders of chivalry: Peter with the Order of St Andrew the First-Called (the oldest and most senior order in Russia, established in the late 1690s; the Tsar was presented with the order in 1703 by its first member, Fiodor Golovin, for the capture of two Swedish vessels in the mouth of the Neva), Catherine with the Order of St Catherine (established especially for women in 1714).

Although 1764 is held to be the date when the imperial museum was founded, the first works of Western European and Classical art were purchased and brought to St Petersburg on the instructions of Peter the Great, and sometimes by him personally. In 1714 and 1715 he sent special agents to Europe whose tasks included the acquisition of artistic treasures for the Russian court.

Predominant among the works brought to Russia in the early eighteenth-century were paintings by Dutch artists, but canvases by Flemish and Italian artists, ancient statues and the creations of contemporary sculptors were also bought. Many of these acquisitions later found their way into the Hermitage collection.

The events of early-eighteenth-century Russian history are commemorated in the very architecture of

The Great Carriage. 1717. **Paris**

The Peter the Great Hall. **Part of the ceiling**

the Winter Palace. In 1833–34, Montferrand produced a memorial hall dedicated to Peter the Great as the creator of the Russian Empire, military commander and founder of St Petersburg. (The hall was restored by Stasov after the 1837 fire.) The walls are lined with Lyons velvet embroidered with silver two-headed eagles — the Russian imperial coat-of-arms — and laurel branches. Two-headed eagles, supplemented by figures of Glory and martial attributes, also serve as the main motif in the ceiling painting, produced in the *grisaille* technique with gold hatching. White marble Corinthian columns flank the niche containing a large painting by the Italian artist Jacopo Amiconi (1675–1752). This allegorical work depicts Glory leading Peter the Great by the hand. The upper part of the architectural frame of the painting incorporates Peter's

monogram in Latin letters, a motif repeated extensively in the decoration of the hall: on the white marble panels that support the columns and pilasters, in the corners of the velvet panels and in the ceiling painting.

The walls are adorned with two battle scenes painted by Barnaba Medici (1778–1859) and Pietro Scotti (1768–1837/38), depicting Peter the Great at Lesnaya and Poltava, important battles in the Northern War (which ended in 1721 with a Russian victory).

The Peter the Great Hall was intended for receptions and was alternatively known as the Small Throne Room. Standing on a dais in the niche is the throne produced for Peter's niece Anna Ioannovna in 1731–32 by the English craftsman Nicholas Clausen. It stood in the Throne Room of that Empress's palace which has not survived. The chair and the footrest were made of pine and decorated with gilded hammered silver. The red velvet upholstery covering the throne today is nineteenth-century work. It is embroidered with two-headed eagles and depictions of St George in silver and different-coloured silks.

Silver was used to make the side tables and all the lighting devices that still adorn the hall today — standard lamps, wall lights and chandelier. They are all the work of St Petersburg craftsmen. The decoration is complemented by a parquet floor containing a large number of precious varieties of wood.

One of the largest halls in the Winter Palace is the Armorial Hall with a floor area of over 1,000 square metres (10,000 square feet). Stasov, who designed it, used the coats-of-arms of Russian provinces in the decoration. The emblems still feature on the gilded bronze chandeliers, but in the nineteenth century they could also be found on the shafts of spears held by sculpted warriors. Groups of them, created by Julius Streichenberg (1814–1863), were placed by the end walls, alongside the portico-doorways into the Peter the Great and Picket Halls. The paired Corinthian columns and pilasters, highly unusually in being gilded all over, create an impression of emphatic monumentality and a somewhat ponderous pomp in a hall intended for ceremonies involving large numbers of people.

The Armorial Hall links the Peter the Great Hall with the Gallery of 1812, created by Carlo Rossi (1775/77–1849) as a memorial to Russia's military glory. The gallery is still one of the best known rooms in the palace. It was formally opened on 25 December 1826 in the presence of generals, other officers and soldiers

The Peter the Great Hall. **Architect Auguste Montferrand, 1833–34**

of the guards who had taken part in the war against Napoleon. After a service in the Large Palace Church, the guardsmen marched through the gallery.

The walls here are lined with 329 portraits of generals who took part in the campaigns of 1812–14. The list of those who were to be honoured in this way was drawn up by the General Staff.). They were painted by George Dawe (1781–1829), an Englishman invited to Russia by Alexander I, with the assistance of Wilhelm Golike (1802–1848) and Alexander Poliakov (1801–1835). Some of the generals were painted in Moscow by the celebrated Russian artist Vasily Tropinin (1776–1857) and then copied by Dawe in the format chosen for the gallery. Work on the portraits began in 1819 and was completed in 1828.

One of the most famous and popular generals in the Russian army that defied the French invasion was Prince Piotr Bagration. Despite his princely title and an ancestry going back to ancient kings of Georgia, Bagration enjoyed neither significant wealth nor connections at the start of his career and entered the army in the ranks. That did not prevent him from becoming the hero of twenty wars and campaigns, participating in 150 battles and earning the favour of both Suvorov and Kutuzov. Napoleon himself called Bagration "the finest general in the Russian army". During the key battle of the 1812 campaign, which took place on 26 August by the village of Borodino, west of Moscow, the Prince commanded the second army which stood on the Russian left flank and was fatally wounded. Bagration died on 12 September 1812 in the village of Simy in Vladimir province. Later his mortal remains were returned to the Borodino battlefield. Dawe painted the portrait of the general in the gallery from an original executed during his lifetime.

The Armorial Hall. **Part of the interior**

The Armorial Hall. **Architect Vasily Stasov, 1837–39**

28

Laurits Regner Tuxen. *The Wedding of Nicholas II and Alexandra Fiodorovna.* 1898

drawings that had survived from the previous century as well as the information of those who knew the place well. Working from Stasov's drawings, P. Cretan and the Tarasov brothers recreated the carved wooden

The Large Palace Church. **Architect Francesco Bartolommeo Rastrelli, 1754–62 Watercolour by Eduard Hau**

iconostasis, the altar canopy and the pulpit. The sculpture and decorative ornamentation was restored (with the extensive use of *papier-mâché*) by Denio Adt, Vasily Demuth-Malinovsky (1779–1846), Piotr Svintsov (died late 1840s), Julius Streichenberg and the Dylev brothers, master stuccoers. The appearance of the church together with a number of other interiors in the palace was recorded in the 1860s by the artist Eduard Hau (1807–1887).

Nicolas Poussin. *Tancred and Erminia.* **1630s**

The Large Church was intended for festive services. It was used, for example, on 14 November 1894 for the marriage of Nicholas II to Princess Alice (Alix) of Hesse-Darmstadt, who became Empress Alexandra Fiodorovna. In the Danish artist Laurits Tuxen's depiction of the ceremony we can see part of the church immediately before the iconostasis: a large window with heavy crimson drapes, gilded moulding on the walls, gilded wall-lights and icons.

The rooms in the southern part of the Winter Palace, overlooking Palace Square, were decorated in a new way after the 1837 fire. In the second half of the eighteenth century these were the living apartments of Catherine the Great, but nothing remains of the interiors of her day. The whole suite of connected rooms is occupied by a display of French art dating from the fifteenth to eighteenth centuries, including paintings, sculpture, fine furniture, bronze, porcelain and tapestries. Catherine avidly acquired the works of French painters for her picture gallery and in doing so laid the foundations of one of the largest sections in the collection.

Seventeenth-century painting is represented by the works of court artists (Simon Vouet, Sebastian Bourdon, Charles Le Brun), the remarkable master of the peasant genre Louis Le Nain (1593–1648) and the outstanding landscape painter Claude Lorrain (1600–1682).

The pride of this collection are the paintings of the great Nicolas Poussin (1594–1665). As a Classicist Poussin created in his works as perfect world peopled with ideal heroes ready for great deeds.

In one of his masterpieces, *Tancred and Erminia* (1630s), the artist depicts just such a great act performed for the sake of love. The subject, taken from the sixteenth-century Italian poet Torquato Tasso's celebrated epic *Jerusalem Delivered*, is the story of

The suite of rooms housing the display of 15th–18th-century French Art

Jean-Baptiste Siméon Chardin. *Still Life with Attributes of the Arts*. 1766

an Eastern princess who falls in love with a European crusader knight and uses her hair to bind his wounds.

The eighteenth century is superbly represented through works by the most outstanding artists. First and foremost, that means the canvases of one of France's greatest painters, Antoine Watteau (1684–1721) and the pictures of Jacques Honoré Fragonard, one of that country's most charming artists.

An entire hall is devoted to the art of the Rococo. It includes paintings by François Boucher (1703–1770), arguably the finest exponent of the style, as well as Rococo furniture and sculpture. In the centre of the hall is the waggish *Threatening Cupid* by Etienne Maurice Falconet (1716–1791).

Jean-Baptiste Chardin (1699–1779), one of the leading artists of the Age of Enlightenment as the eighteenth century is often called, is represented by two genre paintings (*Laundress* and *Saying Grace*) and the *Still Life with Attributes of the Arts* (1766) that was commissioned from him by Catherine II for the St Petersburg Academy of Arts.

That work contains symbolic allusions to painting (a palette and brushes), sculpture (a statuette of Mercury by Jean-Baptiste Pigalle, architecture (blueprints and draughtsmen's instruments), artistic crafts (a jug) and graphic art (a bundle of engravings) — those lofty spheres of human activity in which the artist is called to serve. And for that service he receives public recognition and awards such as the medal depicted in the foreground.

Jean-Antoine Houdon
Voltaire Seated. **1781. Marble**

33

Bureau. By David Roentgen

One of the most famous sculptural works of the Age of Enlightenment is *Voltaire Seated* (1781) by Jean-Antoine Houdon (1741–1828). This three-dimensional portrait was commissioned by Catherine II, who corresponded regularly with the great philosopher.

Houdon produced a vivid image of an aged, decrepit body, that is nonetheless filled with the greatness, wisdom and subtle irony of a genius. The monument-

ality of the work, the precise integral lines and marble clothing reminiscent of ancient drapery accord with the Classical traditions which came to dominate art in the last decades of the eighteenth century.

This kind of art is also displayed in the White Hall where we find landscapes with Classical ruins painted

The White Hall. Architect Alexander Briullov, 1837–41

Thomas Gainsborough. *Portrait of a Lady in Blue*. **1770s**

famous works in the collection. This canvas with its refined execution and elegiac mood is the only Gainsborough in the Hermitage.

Joshua Reynolds (1723–1792), the first president of the Royal Academy, earned fame both as a superb portraitist and as a master of historical painting.

To a commission from the Russian Empress he produced the monumental allegorical work *The Infant Hercules Strangling a Serpent* (1786–88), while for Prince Potemkin he painted *The Continence of Scipio Africanus* (1788–89).

Another aspect of Reynolds's work is to be seen in the more intimate painting *Cupid Untying the Girdle of Venus* (1788). The image in this exquisitely executed canvas is full of a playful coquettishness in the spirit of the "gallant age".

On show together the paintings there are some superb examples of English decorative and applied art, but part of the Hermitage's stocks are displayed apart from the main English section.

The Hermitage's collection of seventeenth- and eighteenth-century German painting is the largest in

Europe outside Germany, but the art of the preceding two centuries is represented by a relatively small number of paintings and sculptures. They do, however, include some first-rate works, among which pride of place must go to those of one of the leading artists of the German Renaissance — Lucas Cranach the Elder (1472–1553).

His *Female Portrait* (1526), depicting a lady from aristocratic circles, embodies the ideal of beauty fashionable at the court of the Elector of Saxony, where Cranach was court painter. This may not be a likeness of a particular person, but rather a collective idealized image.

The portrait, which accounts for a considerable part of Cranach's output, was one of the most popular genres in German Renaissance art. It is represented in the Hermitage by a number of works by noted artists — Ambrosius Holbein, Bartel Bruyn the Elder, Christoph Amberger and Georg Penz.

The collection of fifteenth- and sixteenth-century plastic art includes both the wooden reliefs typical of Germany and sculpture in the round. One of the finest items in this collection is a fifteenth-century stone *Lamentation*.

Again the paintings and sculpture are complemented by a display of decorative and applied art. Porcelain and silver by German masters are included in special exhibitions located in various parts of the Winter Palace.

The display of French nineteenth- and twentieth-century art is situated in the second-floor rooms in the southern part of the Winter Palace. The rooms over-looking the courtyard are occupied by the paintings and sculpture of the first half of the nineteenth century. Despite some undeniable gaps in the collection, it provides an introduction to some of the leading exponents of Classicism, Romanticism and Realism.

Jacques-Louis David (1748–1825), the head of the Classical school, is represented by the Empire-period painting *Sappho and Phaon* (1811); his favourite pupil,

Joshua Reynolds
Cupid Untying the Girdle of Venus. **1788**

Lucas Cranach the Elder
Female Portrait. **1526**

Claude Monet. *Lady in the Garden. Sainte-Adresse*. 1867

Alfred Sisley. *Village on the Seine*. 1872

Sainte-Adresse (1867) — was produced at the start of the artist's path to "daylight painting" with its vibrating air and bright colour-scheme, but even in this canvas sunlight was already a key element.

The 1872 landscape *Village on the Seine* by Alfred Sisley is also full of sunlight and the play of coloured shadows. A subtle and intimate lyricist, Sisley more than any other was able to convey the charm of the provincial countryside.

Abandoning the studio, the Impressionists painted their works directly outdoors — *en plein air*. Their aim was to convey the instantaneous visual impression of a setting, and one of their favourite motifs, reflections in water, became a sort of symbol for the inconstancy of the visible world. The later paintings by Monet and Sisley in the Hermitage collection are splendid examples of "an instant in the life of nature" arrested on the canvas.

The portraitist Auguste Renoir (1841–1919) is represented by works from various periods. One of his most outstanding creations is the *Portrait of Jeanne Samary* (1878). This actress at the Comédie Française was one of the artist's favourite models, closely embodying the "Renoir type". The work was executed with the virtuoso handling of the subtlest nuances of colour and free use of separate brushstrokes that characterized Renoir's mature manner.

The collection also introduces us to the urban landscapes of Camille Pissarro (1830–1903) who sang the praises of Paris and the pastels of Edgar Degas (1834–1917).

A separate room is given over to the work of the greatest sculptor of the Impressionist era — Auguste Rodin (1840–1917).

Post-Impressionism is represented by its most vivid figures: Cézanne, Van Gogh and Gauguin. Each of these painters passed through Impressionism and went on to find his own individual path.

We can study the painting of Paul Cézanne (1839–1906) from works belonging to a variety of genres (landscape, portrait, still life and interior) and to different periods from *Girl at the Piano* of 1866 to *Mont Sainte Victoire* created about 1900.

One of the finest still lifes Paul Cézanne ever produced is his famous painting *Still Life with Drapery* (*ca.* 1899). Its theme, the constructional logic, the heroic spirit of elevated "eternal" life as opposed to

Auguste Renoir
Portrait of the Actress Jeanne Samary. **1878**

the fleeting and transient, express this artist's "Classical" vision and concept of the world. Cézanne's advice to paint with "cubes, cones and spheres" (that is to say, to seek out the simple, "fundamental" forms) later became a slogan for the Cubists.

The four paintings by Vincent van Gogh (1853–1890) date from the last three years of his life. Two of them — *Ladies of Arles. Memories of the Garden at Etten* (1888) and *The Arena in Arles* (1888) were painted in Provence, in the south of France, where the intensely resonant colours staggered the artist's imagination.

Paul Cézanne. *Still Life with Drapery. Ca.* **1889**

One of his masterpieces is *The Lilac Bush* (1889). In this painting, full of vital force and at the same time with dramatic tension, van Gogh's incomparable temperament. It expressed itself in the extreme intensity of the colours, in the dynamic treatment of space and in the animated texture like ploughed-up earth.

The romantic perception of life held by Paul Gauguin (1848–1903) created the image of a primordial harmonious world generated by the canvases of his Tahitian period. One of the visions of that world is *Nave nave moa (The Miraculous Spring)* of 1894. In this work the artist endows natural life unspoiled by civilization with traditional Christian symbols: the halo around the head of one of the Tahitian women, the apple — the fruit of paradise — held by the second girl and the lily a simple for the purity of the Virgin Mary.

Flowing lines and flat abstracted patches of colour subordinated to a single rhythm are expressive elements in the distinctive style of Gauguin and his followers that came to be known as Synthetism.

The display here also includes paintings in the Pointillist technique (tiny dots of pure colour) by the Neo-Impressionists Paul Signac (1863–1935) and Henri Edmond Cross (1856–1910), as well as canvases by the Primitivist Henri "Douannier" Rousseau (1844–1910).

A separate room is occupied by the works of the Nabis, a group who took their name from the Hebrew for "prophet" and who represent a sort of link between Post-Impressionism and twentieth-century art, particularly the *art nouveau*: Maurice Denis (1870–1943), Pierre Bonnard (1864–1947), Edouard Vuillard (1868–1940), Xavier Roussel (1867–1944) and the Swiss Felix Valloton (1865–1925).

Early-twentieth-century art is represented by the work of artists belonging to two main tendencies — Cubism and Fauvism. First and foremost, Picasso and Matisse.

The paintings of Henri Matisse (1869–1954) fill several rooms. He produced a whole series of monumental canvases for Sergei Shchukin, who was one of his main patrons at that time. These works include the

Vincent van Gogh. *The Lilac Bush*. 1889

Paul Gauguin. *Nave nave moa (The Miraculous Spring)*. 1894

45

Pablo Picasso. *Peasant Woman*. 1908

celebrated *Red Room* (1908). Conceived originally as *Harmony in Blue* and painted in a colour-scheme appropriate to that, the canvas was reworked by the artist in pursuit of more expressive colour.

Matisse painted a pair of monumental works — *Dance* (1909–10) and *Music* (1910) — specially for the stairwell of Shchukin's mansion in Moscow.

A significant portion of the twentieth-century painting collection is made up of works by other Fauves ("wild beasts"). Like their leader Henri Matisse, these artists (Albert Marquet, Kees van Dongen, Maurice Vlaminck and Georges Rouault) made colour the chief protagonist of their works, yet each of them had a distinctive manner of painting. The work of Pablo Picasso (1881–1973) is represented chiefly

by paintings of the Blue and, especially, Cubist periods.

One of the high spots of the blue series is the monumental *Two Sisters (The Visit)* from 1902.

The yearning to get back to "fundamentals" that the artist found in primitive art, an urge that developed into Cubism, expresses itself in the forms, simplified down to their geometric prototypes, making up the figure of the *Peasant Woman* (1908). The model for this painting (an another with the same name, but different composition) was the owner of a house in the country where Picasso stayed. According to Picasso: "An artist should observe nature, but never confuse it with painting. Nature can only be translated into painting through signs."

Henri Matisse. *The Red Room.* **1908**

The display of paintings by these great figures of twentieth-century art is supplemented with sculptural works by Matisse and ceramics by Picasso.

This series of rooms also contains pieces by two of the century's greatest sculptors — Aristide Maillol (1861–1944) and Emile-Antoine Bourdelle (1861–1929).

The parallel suite of rooms on the courtyard side is used to display nineteenth- and twentieth-century works from Western Europe (apart from France) and America.

The collection of twentieth-century art is being actively enlarged at the moment with paintings and sculptures by contemporary artists.

Among the rooms that provide us with an idea of the appearance of the living quarters in the palace in the nineteenth century are the Golden Reception Room, Crimson Study, Boudoir and Green Dining-Room. These were created in the 1830s–60s and reflect the typical tendency in Russian interior decoration of that time to borrow from the artistic traditions of the past, the deliberate combination of elements belonging to different architectural styles.

One of the first to use this approach was the architect Alexander Briullov. In the late 1830s and early 1840s

→

The Golden Reception Room. **Architects: Alexander Briullov, 1841; Andrei Stakenschneider, 1850s**

The Golden Reception Room. A fireplace

The Crimson Study. Architect Andrei Stakenschneider, 1860s

he decorated private apartments in the Winter Palace for the family of Emperor Nicholas I. They included the Golden Reception Room intended for Grand Duchess Maria Alexandrovna, the wife of the Emperor's eldest son, the future Alexander II. In the 1850s another architect, Andrei Stakenschneider (1802–1865), modified the decoration of the room and some changes were also made later.

The walls and piers of the room are decorated with fine relief ornament including tendrils and palmettes and completely gilded over. Gilding was also used on the elaborately patterned ceiling ornament and the massive carved cornices above the eight windows. In the centre of each of these cornices is a cartouche containing the Grand Duchess's monogram — *MA*. The same monogram features in the decoration of the

gilded furniture. The whole set was produced to Stakenschneider's design. The bright upholstery of the armchairs and sofas intensified still further the colourful richness of the interior. The same role is played by the drapes at the windows and doors. The decoration of the room is enhanced by a fireplace finished in white marble and adorned by a mosaic panel depicting Classical ruins.

The Crimson Study (or Crimson Drawing-Room), which retains the appearance of the 1860s designed by Stakenschneider, was also created for Maria Alexandrovna, who was by then the Empress. The main decorative element in this interior are large woven wall panels (the colour of the silk gave the study its name) enclosed in moulded frames. Since the room was intended for music-making, the pattern of the material features musical notes and instruments.

The flatness of the silk panels forms an effective contrast with the three-dimensional quality of the broad moulded frieze at the top of the walls: brackets linked in pairs by gilded garlands of flowers alternate with cartouches filled with moulded *putti* and musical instruments. The extensive use of reliefs in the decoration of the room reaches its limit in high relief figures of cupids adorning the frame of the mirror above the fireplace and supporting a cartouche containing the *MA* monogram of the study's mistress.

Today the Crimson Study is used to display the collection of porcelain and pottery including items from the celebrated *Green Frog Service* created in Britain by Josiah Wedgwood and Thomas Bentley. This lead-glazed earthenware service was produced in 1773–74 to a commission from Catherine the Great for a palace under construction just outside St Petersburg, on the road to her beloved summer estate of Tsarskoye Selo. Since the local Finnish name for the spot where the palace was being built was Kekerekeksinen, meaning "frog marsh", each item of the service bears a green frog in a frame shaped like a heraldic shield. (The palace, of which little has survived, was soon renamed to commemorate the Russian naval victory over the Turks at Chesme.) The service, intended for fifty people, comprised 944 pieces (of which 770 still exist), decorated with 1,222 views of England, Scotland and Wales painted in tones of brown and black against a cream-coloured background.

The service was made in Staffordshire at Wedgwood's famous *Etruria* factory founded in 1769. From there it was sent south to London, to Chelsea where a team of about thirty craftsmen painted the pieces under Bentley's direction.

A large portion of the depictions are of country estates and parks, but there is also a whole series devoted to London, the surrounding area and the River Thames. The artists worked from engravings, oil-paintings and watercolours, as well as in some instances drawings that were specially made at the relevant locations for this purpose.

The service had a large number of dinner and desert plates intended for several successive courses ("spares" were included in the total to replace any breakage that occurred in use). There were also soup

The Green Frog Service. **1773–74. By Josiah Wedgwood**

tureens, large oval dishes with lids for game birds, round and oval dishes for meat and fish, sauce-boats, salad-bowls, ice-cream dishes (with a complex four-part structure), special dishes for syllabubs and stewed fruit, bottle and glass holders, and any number of other items of different design and purpose reflecting the tastes, etiquette and culinary peculiarities of the eighteenth century. At the same time, due to the refined simplicity of its forms and the virtuoso decoration, the *Green Frog Service* is one of the masterpieces of English pottery. Every item in it is highly practical, well thought-out and convenient to use.

The living apartments of Maria Fiodorovna also included the Boudoir, created in 1853 to the design of the architect Harald Bosse (1812–1894), using the shapes and decorative elements of Rococo interiors. Following the eighteenth-century fashion, an alcove was installed, separated from the main part of the room by an elaborate arch adorned with marble caryatids and a bronze open-work grille. Rich pomegranate-coloured material was specially commissioned for the Boudoir from the Courtier factory in France. It was used not only for the upholstery of the sofas and armchairs, and for the curtains, but also to line the walls. The cloth panels are framed with carved and gilded wood forming elements of a complex pattern. The decoration of the room is completed by mirrors, a marble fireplace, painted insets above the doors and a gilded bronze chandelier.

Bosse's interior creates the impression of a emphatic, even somewhat excessive decorativeness, something highly typical of the design of palace interiors in the latter part of the nineteenth century.

The Green Dining-Room, where Staken-schneider's 1850 decoration has survived virtually intact, also belonged to Maria Alexandrovna's apartments. As in the Boudoir, the design here imitates the Rococo style with its extensive use of stucco, sculpture, paintings, and mirrors, turning the walls into decorative panels of sorts. Instead of the gilding traditionally used in palace interiors at that time, however, all the relief elements were covered

***Boudoir*. Part of the decoration**

with slightly pink English whitewash that forms a refined combination with the pale green of the walls. Green material was also used to upholster the furniture. A few pieces of bronze — chandelier, candelabra and clock — created additional colour accents. The room had no windows as it was created in place of an earlier internal staircase, but an oval metal frame decorated with cast bronze was set in the ceiling and through its panes of matte glass diffused daylight entered the room.

The Rococo was a repeated source of inspiration for nineteenth-century architects. Alexander Krasovsky (1848–1923) again drew upon that era towards the end of the century. It was under his direction that the last reconstruction work in the living quarters of the Winter Palace was carried out. In the 1890s, rooms in the protruding north-western part of

the building were converted for the heir to the throne, soon to become Nicholas II. In these apartments the last Emperor, Empress Alexandra Fiodorovna and their daughters lived for nine years. (In 1904 the family left the residence in the capital for ever and lived permanently at Tsarskoye Selo.) Two of the rooms have retained their decoration down to the present — the Small Dining-Room and the Gothic Library.

Krasovsky imitated the Rococo style in the interior of the Small Dining-Room. The walls are ornamented

$\rightarrow$

The Green Dining-Room.
Architect Andrei Stakenschneider, 1850

The Small Dining-Room.
Architect Alexander Krasovsky, 1890s

53

with typical scrolls, garlands and roses. They frame four Russian-made tapestries of the mid-eighteenth century, three of which (*Asia*, *America* and *Africa*) belong to the *Parts of the World* series. The tapestries were woven by craftsmen of the St Petersburg factory, the oldest in Russia, having been founded in 1717. A further adornment of the room is the crystal chandelier made in England which incorporates a clockwork musical mechanism.

In creating the interior of the library, Krasovsky turned his attention to Gothic architecture. The two main materials used in the decoration of the room — dark carved wood and red leather with gold tooling — set each other off every well creating an atmosphere of Spartan grandeur. The main element of the interior are the carved bookcases adorned with typical Gothic ornament (lancet arches, rosettes, trefoils and so on). The same devices were used in the decoration of the banisters on the stairs leading up to the gallery and the balustrade of the gallery that contains a second tier of bookcases reaching almost to the ceiling. The decoration of the library was complemented by large tables and lecterns, plain chairs and armchairs. All the joinery and carving work for the library was carried out by the craftsmen of N.F. Svirsky's furniture factory.) The Library as an interior is not only an example of fine artistic taste, but also of carefully calculated functionality.

The Library contains an immense fireplace that was an invariable element in a Gothic interior. Work on creating the fireplace began with the production of a plaster model that was then translated into stone by the decorative sculptor Grazioso Botta (1836–1898). The main element of decoration in the fireplace is its crowning "heraldic beasts" frieze made up of alternating coat-of-arms of the House of Romanov (a gryphon) and Hesse-Darmstadt (a lion).

It was in this room that the prayer service was held when the imperial family moved into their new living quarters in December 1895.

The decoration of the remaining rooms that belonged to the family of the last Tsar have not survived. They were reconstructed and turned into

exhibition halls from 1926 onwards. Today they house a display devoted to Russian interior decoration in the nineteenth century, The furniture and tapestries, bronzework and coloured stone, glass and porcelain illustrate the succession of changing styles in Russian decorative and applied art over the course of the nineteenth century , from the late *Empire* Classicism to the *art nouveau*. Pride of place is taken by the furniture, whose role in the decoration of any interior is decisive. It is no coincidence, therefore, that leading architects were involved in the creation of furniture. The display includes sets devised by Rossi, Briullov, Stakenschneider and others whose designs were worked up by the best workshops (Ivan Bauman's, the Gambs family's) and factories (Friedrich Melzer's, Svirsky's).

The former Silver Drawing-Room (silvered carved garlands of leaves and ribbons were a feature of the original decoration of which only the ceiling painting remains), for example, displays furniture from two palace interiors of the 1820s — a drawing-room and

The Gothic Library.
Part of the interior decoration

The Gothic Library.
Architect Alexander Krasovsky, 1890s

The study set. 1800s–30s. **Poplar and Karelian birch**

a study. Both sets were produced from Rossi's designs in Bauman's workshop: the drawing-room (1817) for the Anichkov Palace on the occasion of the marriage of the future Emperor Nicholas I; the study (1819–22) for the Yelagin Palace.

The items in the drawing-room set are painted white and decorated with appliquéd gilded carving. The slightly rounded backs of the chairs, the lyre-shaped splats in the centre of their backs, and the ornament in the form of rosettes, palmettes, butterflies and so on, splendidly convey the distinctive features of *Empire*-style furniture. The green and gold silk upholstery appeared on the set in the 1880s, when it was moved to the Winter Palace; originally the furniture was adorned with pale blue velvet.

The study set was produced from a timber rarely used in Russian cabinet-making — curly maple

enhanced by bronze appliqué elements. This set included a number of new items, that were introduced at just that time, such as the couch and the bureau.

Poplar and Karelian birch, woods that possesses a warm, golden yellow colour and an unusual texture with darker dividing lines and scattered patches, were used to veneer a number of pieces of early-nineteenth-century furniture now in the display — a sofa, armchairs, a table, a bureau, and a dressing-table with a large mirror in a rectangular frame. When working with Karelian birch and poplar, cabinet-makers strive to bring out to the maximum the natural beauty of the wood which matches so well with the refined simplicity of Classical furniture. Articles from furniture sets with these attractive finishes are placed in a former bedroom.

Sets of furniture for the State Drawing-Room and Study.
Designed by Carlo Rossi, 1817–22

A link between the palace state rooms and the private apartments of the imperial family was the Malachite Room created in the late 1830s to the design of Alexander Briullov for Alexandra Fiodorovna, the wife of Nicholas I. The mineral that gives its name to the hall was a rarity in Russia up until the nineteenth century, but the discovery of rich deposits in the Urals in 1835 made it possible to use it not only for making small decorative items, but even as a finish for architectural elements.

Over two tons of the stone were used in decorating the Malachite Room. It was obtained from the copper mine owned by the Demidov family near Nizhny Tagil. It was used on the columns and pilasters, fireplaces and tables, vases and candlesticks. But this is only a fine "veneer" of malachite: thin plates of the mineral were selected for their pattern and arranged in such a

way that the composition retained the appearance of the natural stone. The malachite was attached with a special adhesive to a base of ordinary stone or metal. The surface of the object was then carefully ground and polished. This technique has come to be known as Russian mosaic. The oldest example in the Malachite Room is the large decorative vase beneath a gilded wooden canopy by the windows. The vase adorned the Winter Palace even before the blaze of 1837. The particular pattern employed on it is known as "mint velvet".

Russian nineteenth-century craftsmen had several other patterns at their disposal. On the columns and

→
The Malachite Room.
Architect Alexander Briullov, 1837–39

The Malachite Room. Articles made of malachite

Cupboard with the "Tropical Forest"
mosaic panel. **1888–92**
Peterhof Lapidary Works

pilasters, for example, there are "ribbons" — the lighter veins extend across the darker background of the stone in a continuous line from the bases to the capitals. The "radial" or "eye" composition looks like the cut trunk of a tree with annual growth-rings, while the "two-sided" or "four-sided" pattern rely for their effect on a symmetrical arrangement of pieces.

The malachite looks particularly striking set off by the white artificial marble walls combined with the gilding covering the bronze vases and capitals of the columns, the frames of the mirrors, the carved doors and the relief ornament on the ceiling (which is made of *papier-mâché*). Additional colour accents are introduced by the crimson upholstery of the furniture. The combination of bright stone, silk and glittering gold in the decoration of the Empress's state drawing-room create an atmosphere of magnificent splendour.

One of the walls in the room is adorned by three painted female figures representing Day, Night and Poetry. They were created by Antonio Vighi (1764–1845). The parquet floor in the Malachite Room was produced from nine different kinds of wood following a design by the architect Nikolai Gornostayev (1853 – after 1917).

The malachite vase that stands in the centre of the room was made to the design of another noted Russian architect, Andrei Voronikhin (1759–1814), early in the nineteenth century. The "mint velvet" bowl of the vase rests on a tripod of gilded bronze featuring three winged figures. The tables in the room with malachite tops, carved and gilded bases were made in 1830 to the design of a third architect — Johann Hallberg (1782–1863).

Display cases in the Malachite Room contain table and mantelpiece ornaments, ink-stands, paperweights and candlesticks all finished with malachite. In these small objects, as on the monumental scale of the architectural interior, the green mineral is effectively combined with gilded bronze.

All the stone-cutting work relating to this room was performed by the craftsmen of the Peterhof Lapidary Works. Their skilled hands and tools created many pieces of decorative and applied art that still adorn the Hermitage today. They used a range of raw materials, many of which were mined in abundant quantities in the Altai and Ural mountains during the nineteenth century. As well as mahogany and gilded bronze the decorative "Tropical Forest" cupboard produced in 1888–92, for example, features a mosaic panel assembled in Peterhof from jasper, lapis-lazuli, malachite, sardonyx, opal, granite and ordinary pebbles from the Crimea.

Alongside the Malachite Room is the Concert Hall, part of the Neva suite of state rooms (all three of which have windows overlooking the river). The hall was created by Giacomo Quarenghi in the 1790s in place of Rastrelli's Anteroom; in the 1830s it was re-constructed by Montferrand, and restored in 1837 by Stasov with a few alterations, chiefly affecting the decoration. The hall was indeed intended for concerts and this is reflected not only in the name, but also in the decoration. The grisaille painting by Barnaba

Vase. **First half of the 19th century Malachite. Peterhof Lapidary Works**

Medici on the cove features allegorical figures and musical instruments. The paired Corinthian columns faced with white plaster carry a cornice adorned by twenty-eight statues depicting the muses by the sculptor Joseph Hermann (1800–1869).

Since 1922 the Concert Hall has been used to display the massive silver tomb of Saint Alexander Nevsky, one of the best known works of Russian Baroque art, brought here from the Alexander Nevsky Monastery.

In 1240 Prince Alexander Yaroslavich of Novgorod defeated the Swedes on the bank of the Neva, a victory that earned him the surname Nevsky. In 1724 the relics of the Prince (who was canonized soon after his death) were transferred from Vladimir to St Petersburg, the city built on lands recovered from the Swedes and placed in the main cathedral of the monastery founded in his honour in 1713.

The Concert Hall. Statues of Muses

In 1745, on the orders of Empress Elizabeth, the daughter of Peter the Great, work began on a monumental tomb to be made of silver. About one and a half tons of the precious metal, mined at Kolyvan in the Altai, was used on the project which took until 1751 to complete.

Among those involved in this undertaking were the artists Georg Groot and Luigi Caravaque, the sculptor Johann Dunker, the master-caster Alessandro Martelli, the carver and engraver Stahlmeyer and the silversmith Deichmann, together with a large team of chasers, engravers, smiths and so on. The entire project was supervised by I. A. Shlater, an official of the mint.

The elaborate ensemble includes a coffin-like reliquary, a pyramid, military attributes and two candlesticks. The reliquary is decorated with chased high-relief depictions of events in Russian thirteenth-century history connected with Prince Alexander Nevsky: the battle on the Neva against the Swedes in 1240, the battle against the knights of the Livonian Order on the ice of Lake Peipus and the liberation of Pskov in 1242. Here too are depictions of the Prince's arrival in the Gorodetsky Monastery after his visit to the Golden Horde, and his death in 1263.

In the centre of the pyramid is a *bas-relief* with an allegory of Faith directing Alexander Nevsky. Higher up are sculptural depictions of angels holding shields that bear the words of a poem by Mikhail Lomonosov (1711–1765) extolling the Prince's services to the Russian nation. The tomb is crowned by a depiction of Alexander Nevsky set against the background of an ermine robe.

A number of interiors in the Winter Palace that now contain museum exhibitions were deliberately reconstructed to make them better suited to the display of various collections. The main palace canteen, for example, situated on the ground floor, was turned into a large exhibition hall in the 1930s. Today it houses one of the displays of the Department of Oriental Culture and Art, devoted to Ancient Egypt.

The earliest exhibits in the display date back to the fifth millennium B.C. — stone weapons found in the Nile delta. Stone was also the material used for the numerous reliefs and statues around the hall that reflect different stages in the development of fine art in Ancient Egypt. Among the best works in this collection are a granite depiction from the Middle Kingdom period, depicting Pharaoh Amenemhat III who lived in the nineteenth century B.C. In this portrait, besides the strict adherence to the established canon so typical of Ancient Egyptian art, one can detect the sculptor's efforts to convey the individual features of his royal subject.

The New Kingdom produced one of the most famous reliefs in the Hermitage collection — the stele of Ipi, major-domo of the pharaoh's palace. It was created in Memphis in the first half of the fourteenth

The Concert Hall
Architect Vasily Stasov, 1837–39

century B.C., a period when Ancient Egyptian art flourished. Ipi is depicted before the god Anubis, the protector of the dead who was conventionally depicted with the head of a jackal. The stele is marked by a combination of monumental composition with decorativeness and emphatically refined lines, something very characteristic for the art of the period.

Another creation of the New Kingdom, in this case from the fifteenth century B.C., is one of the masterpieces of the Hermitage Egyptian collection — a small wooden figure of a youth walking. The somewhat elongated proportions of the body and head, the delicate features of the face, the soft modelling of forms are evidence of the birth of a style that would determine the development of art in the Amarna period, one of the peaks of Ancient Egyptian culture.

Other halls of the Winter Palace were given over to the displays of the Department of Primitive Culture that present numerous archaeological finds dating from the Stone to Iron Ages. Among them are unique fifth- and fourth-century B.C. artefacts created by the early nomads of the Altai discovered during the excavations of the world-famous Pazyryk Valley burial mounds in 1947–49. These rich graves of the local tribal aristocracy had been plundered back in ancient times and their gold treasures were lost. But beneath the great heaps of stones, the permafrost conditions preserved things that never usually come down to us from such distant past — organic materials like wood, leather, felt and woven fabric. In the fifth Pazyryk mound (fifth – fourth century B.C.) archaeologists found beneath a four-metre mound and a layer of logs a pit containing a burial chamber consisting of two frameworks of logs, the smaller (on display) inside the larger. These frames were made of larch trunks and covered with birch-bark sheets; inside was a coffin made from a block of wood holding the mummified bodies of a man and a woman. Here too they found fragments of a white felt

Statue of Pharaoh Amenemhat III.
19th century B.C. Black granite

Room of the Art of Ancient Egypt

The Stele of Ipi. **14th century B.C.**

Striding Youth. **15th century B.C.**

Napped woollen carpet. Fifth Pazyryk Burial-Mound. 5th – 4th-century B.C.

carpet decorated with coloured appliqué patches, part of a little wooden table, a small drum, a sheepskin cushion, and many other items.

Lying alongside the log frames in the grave pit were a felt carpet, a dismantled wooded chariot, four draught-horses and five saddle-horses.

The almost three-metre high birch-wood chariot is in an exceptionally fine state of preservation. Each of the wheels has a diameter of over one and a half metres and has 34 spokes glued in place for extra strength.

The same fifth Pazyryk mound also yielded the world's oldest surviving napped carpet, brought to the Altai from Iran or Central Asia. In order to produce the geometric pattern that adorns the carpet and the borders containing depictions of people and animals the craftsmen had to tie over 1,250,000 knots in the relatively small area of just over 3.5 square metres.

The felt carpet found in the mound was probably local work. It has an area of about 30 square metres and was decorated with appliqué images repeated several times of a goddess seated on a throne and a horseman riding up to her.

The unique finds from the Pazyryk Valley burial mounds are among the most famous exhibits in the museum.

**Chariot. Fifth Pazyryk Burial-Mound.
5th – 4th-centure B.C.**

68

The Small Hermitage. **Facade of the southern pavilion. Architect Yury Velten, 1764–75**

THE SMALL HERMITAGE

The building now known as the Small Hermitage was constructed alongside the Winter Palace between 1764 and 1775. It was designed by two architects: Jean-Baptiste Vallin de la Mothe (1729–1800) and Yury Velten (1730–1801). The new edifice consisted of two pavilions, two galleries and a hanging garden. Here the Empress held her "little hermitages", soirees for her closest confidants. Catherine also devised the rules to be followed at these gatherings that involved theatrical performances and concerts and ended with private dinners. The plays presented included some written by the Empress herself and her courtiers on subjects from Russian history. The galleries of the Small Hermitage were intended for the paintings that grew in numbers continuously during Catherine's reign. The acquisition of Gotzkowsky's collection was followed by the purchase of those of Count Karl Cobenzl (Brussels, 1768), Count Heinrich Brühl (Dresden, 1769), Pierre Crozat (Paris, 1772), Sir Robert Walpole (Houghton Hall, England, 1779), Count Baudoin (Paris, 1781) and a number of other private collections. These acquisitions around Europe were made by the Russian ambassadors as well as special agents. In her purchasing activities Catherine II was advised and assisted by some of her most enlightened contemporaries — Diderot, Grimm and Tronchin. An important role in the formation of the collection was played by the Russian diplomat and scholar Prince Dmitry Golitsyn. (It is due to him that the Hermitage possesses one of its most glorious masterpieces — Rembrandt's *Return of the Prodigal Son*.)

The Small Hermitage. The Hanging Garden

According to the 1774 inventory, the Empress's museum already contained 2,080 paintings, as well as a large collection of drawings, engravings, coins and medals, numerous gems and a cabinet of minerals.

At the same time as the galleries of the Small Hermitage were being constructed, work was proceeding on the Hanging Garden, situated at second-storey level and enclosed by the walls of the galleries and pavilions. A one-and-a-half- to two-metre layer of soil rests on metal sheets attached to the masonry vaults of the ground floor.

In 1856–58 Stakenschneider replaced the eighteenth-century interiors of the northern pavilion with the Pavilion Hall. This room that occupies almost the entire second storey is decorated in a manner that combines elements of Ancient, Moorish and Renais-

sance architecture. Chiselled marble columns, light arcades, gilded grilles, decorative niches and "fountains of tears" endowed it with a special elegance. The exquisite architectural forms are emphasized by the use of many chandeliers, large and small, with individual drops shaped like oak-leaves. The floor is adorned by a mosaic panel depicting the head of the Gorgon Medusa and scenes from Classical mythology: the battle between the Lapiths and the Centaurs, and tritons and naiads playing with hippocampi. The panel was created in Rome in 1847–51. Its prototype was a mosaic that decorated the floor of the baths in the Ancient town of Ocriculum.

→
The Pavilion Hall.
Architect Andrei Stakenschneider, 1856–58

The Pavilion Hall. **Decorative niche and "Fountain of Tears"**

Now the Pavilion Hall houses a display of decorative tables with mosaic tops of different minerals and coloured glass created by Italian eighteenth- and nineteenth-century craftsmen. This is also the home of the famous Peacock Clock designed by the Englishman James Cox, one of the most skilled clock-makers of the day.

The Pavilion Hall.
Architect Andrei Stakenschneider, 1856–58

Bought by Prince Potemkin in 1780 and brought to St Petersburg in pieces, the elaborate timepiece was reassembled only in 1792 by Ivan Kulibin (1735–1818), himself the author of many complex mechanisms. When the clock strikes, the gilded peacock "comes to life": it spreads its tail, turns and bows to the spectators. The owl in a round cage alongside turns its head and blinks its eyes, while the cockerel crows. The mechanism is still in working order today.

The Old Hermitage. **The room housing the display of 13th – 14th-century Italian Art. Decoration designed by Andrei Stakenschneider**

THE OLD HERMITAGE

One more building was soon added for the rapidly expanding collections "in line with" the Small Hermitage. It was put up between 1771 and 1778 to the design of Yury Velten. Originally known as the Large Hermitage, it has been called the Old Hermitage since the construction of the New Hermitage is the middle of the nineteenth century.

The facade is in the same Classical style as the neighbouring Small Hermitage, but it looks more austere and restrained.

In the mid-1800s the building was reconstructed by Stakenschneider due to the creation of the New Hermitage. The first (Oval) hall was replaced by the Council Staircase. Surviving from the original decoration is the ceiling painting *The Virtues Presenting Russian Youths to Minerva* by the French artist Gabriel François

Doyen (1726–1806). The name of the staircase arose from the fact that the Council of State used to meet on the ground floor of the Old Hermitage. Many collections were transferred to the new museum building while the rooms here became an extension of the living quarters of the Winter Palace. He decorated them in the spirit of the day, drawing on the styles of the past. It is his interiors that have survived down to the present.

The Old Hermitage now contains displays of Italian art from the thirteenth to sixteenth centuries, the age of the Renaissance.

The first hall presents works that belong to the Proto-Renaissance period, when artists still retained many traditions of the Middle Ages, but new features were already emerging in their work — the beginnings of a new system of imagery and depiction.

The earliest exhibit here is a processional cross bearing an image of the crucified Christ, executed in the spirit of

Byzantine icon-painting by Ugolino di Tedice, a Pisan artist of the second half of the thirteenth century. This is presently the only authenticated signed work by the master.

One of the finest examples of Late Gothic art is the *Madonna* from an *Annunciation* by one of the greatest Siennese artists, Simone Martini (*ca.* 1284–1344). The elongated proportions of the delicate, exquisite figure, its refined outline, the flat patches of colour and tooled gilded background are typical Gothic devices, but the soft poetic mood and the natural femininity of the *Madonna* make her a more earthly image than the majestic mediaeval Queens of Heaven.

The display of fifteenth-century art (Early Renaissance) includes works by Fra Beato Angelico da Fiesole (*ca.* 1400–1455) — among them a rare museum exhibit: a fragment of a fresco, Fra Filippo Lippi (*ca.* 1406–1469), Sandro Botticelli (1455–1510) and his finest pupil Filippino Lippi (*ca.* 1457–1504), Pietro Perugino (*ca.* 1450–1523), the teacher of Raphael, and many other noted figure of the period.

The halls also contain works of decorative and applied art (fabrics, *cassoni* chests) and sculpture.

The largest hall in the Neva suite is decorated in imitation of the "grand style" of French seventeenth-century art, which is particularly effective due to the abundant use of gilding. The doors are finished in the Boulle technique with a pattern of tortoiseshell and gilded bronze. Above the doors are stucco-work portraits of Russian field marshals, while the upper parts of the walls are enlivened by painted panels depicting Classical gods. Four of the panels are the work of the noted St Petersburg artist and academician Fiodor Bruni (1799–1875).

This hall is used to display the two works in the Hermitage by the great Leonardo da Vinci (1452–1519). They represent a substantial part of his artistic legacy, since around the world there are only some fourteen paintings left by that Renaissance genius.

The *Madonna and a Child* (1490–91) acquired for the Hermitage in 1865 from the Milanese Dukes of Litta has gone down in art history under the name of its former owners. Executed when Leonardo was a mature artist, it belongs to the High Renaissance when the image of an ideally beautiful human being and a world filled with harmony were being created on the basis of abstract knowledge and conceptions. The Virgin with a severe Classical profile and a barely noticeable smile

Simone Martini
The Madonna from an *Annunciation*. **14th century**

at the corners of her lips breast-feeding the Christ-Child is an embodiment of the wonder of maternity, the epitome of spiritual purity and physical perfection.

In 1914 the museum acquired the *Madonna with a Flower* (1478), which was then owned by the family of the noted architect Leonty Benois (hence the second name — *The Benois Madonna*). This is an early work by the artist that still retains the genre quality of the Early Renaissance. The image of the young Virgin is full of living charm and the mood of the painting is one of delight in earthly motherhood.

→
The Neva enfilade of the Old Hermitage
Architect Andrei Stakenschneider, 1851–60

The Leonardo da Vinci Hall
Architect Andrei Stakenschneider, 1851–60

Leonardo da Vinci. *The Litta Madonna (Madonna and a Child)*. 1490–91

→

Francesco Melzi. *Flora*

Leonardo da Vinci
The Benois Madonna (Madonna with a Flower). **1478**

Cesare da Sesto. *The Holy Family with Saint Catherine*

Displayed in the adjoining room are painting, many of which are reminiscent of Leonardo's work in both the manner and the character of the image. These were produced by the great Florentine's pupils, the best of whom managed to absorb what the master could teach them while retaining their own individuality.

The Holy Family with Saint Catherine, a work by Cesare da Sesto (1477–1523) acquired back in the eighteenth century, was long believed to be by Leonardo himself. It was admired as the creation of the great master by many connoisseurs of painting, including Stendhal who considered this *Holy Family* the finest thing he had produced. Despite the corrected attribution, the painting has lost none of its fine qualities.

Francesco Melzi (1493– *ca.* 1570), Leonardo's favourite pupil, is represented by a work that creates an image of the Classical goddess of spring and protectress of plants. *Flora* is one of two authenticated works by Melzi that are currently known. This work too was attributed to Leonardo. The similarity to his teacher's manner can be detected in the female type, in her mysterious romantic smile and the airy *chiaroscuro* (light and shade) that subtly models shapes.

One of Leonardo's most talented followers was Andrea del Sarto (1486–1531), creator of the *Madonna and Child with Saints Catherine, Elizabeth and John the Baptist* (mid-1510s) that bears the master's signature.

The last hall in the Old Hermitage is devoted to the work of the Mannerists, who devised new approaches to colour, composition and symbolism.

Rosso Fiorentino (1494–1540) and Jacopo Pontormo (1494–1557), members of the first generation of Florentine Mannerists, were pupils of del Sarto, but their madonnas seem strange and unusual, far removed from their teacher's images.

The inner suite of rooms that runs parallel to the Neva enfilade contains one of the most complete and striking parts of the Italian collection — the works of Venetian fifteenth- and

Titian. *Christ Carrying the Cross*. **1560s**

Titian. *Repentant Mary Magdalene*. **1560s**

sixteenth-century artists. Paintings predominate in these rooms, but the display also includes marble decorative reliefs, small-scale plastic art and splendid products of the artistic crafts (furniture, bronze, fabrics, lace, enamel and the celebrated Venetian glass).

The central role in this section is played by the works of Giorgione (*ca.* 1478 – 1510) and Titian (1485/90–1576).

Giorgione's *Judith* is one of the Hermitage's best known paintings. The apocryphal tale of the daring act performed by this young Jewish woman who made her way from a besieged city into the enemy camp and killed Holofernes the commander was very popular in the Renaissance era, an age that valued civic virtues.

The Venetian artist depicted Judith in a victorious pose, her foot resting on the severed head of Holofernes. She has accomplished a heroic deed, but the triumphal spirit is softened by Judith's calm femininity and the untroubled mood of the landscape.

The display includes one further work by Giorgione, a *Madonna and Child*.

Titian's long artistic career is represented by eight paintings of different genres — portrait, mythological and religious subjects.

A younger contemporary of Giorgione and a continuer of the traditions he established, Titian was the most brilliant colourist of the Venetian school, in which colour became the foremost means of expression.

His *Repentant Mary Magdalene* (1560s) is a splendid example of unfettered painting and a complex use of colour. This Gospel figure whose moral exploit lay in withdrawing from a sinful worldly life into solitude embodies not only lofty spirituality, but also sensual corporeal beauty in the Venetian taste.

In *Christ Carrying the Cross* (1560s), a painting from the same period, the image of Jesus is full of the nobility of the martyr bearing the burden of suffering with dignity.

One of the most famous masterpieces by Titian is *The Martyrdom of Saint Sebastian*. This

Giorgione. *Judith*

The Raphael Loggias. **Detail of painting**

painting which the artist produced at the end of his life is fascinating for the boldness of his manner and the astonishing virtuoso execution.

The Venetian rooms also include works by such outstanding artists as Cima da Conegliano (*ca.* 1459 – *ca.* 1517), Palma the Elder (*ca.* 1480–1528), Lorenzo Lotto (*ca.* 1480–1556), Sebastiano del Piombo (1485–1547) and Paolo Veronese (1528–1588).

THE RAPHAEL LOGGIAS

The Raphael Loggias is a separate building that was with time incorporated into the New Hermitage complex. It is a copy of an entire piece of architecture — a gallery in the Vatican Palace in Rome built in the early sixteenth century by the architect Donato Bramante (*ca.* 1444–1514) and painted by the pupils of the great Raphael (1483–1520) from designs by the master and under his direction.

In 1775 Catherine the Great obtained Italian engravings depicting the loggias and reproducing the frescoes in the gallery and she formed the desire to possess copies of the entire cycle of paintings. In 1778 a group of artists led by Christopher Unterberger, a Tyrolean painter resident in Rome, set about copying the paintings, but using egg-tempera paints on canvas rather than the original fresco technique. In 1787 the canvases were brought to St Petersburg.

Meanwhile the idea had arisen to house the paintings in a copy of their setting in the papal residence. The block was designed by Giacomo Quarenghi who began work on it in the summer of 1783, at the same time as the Hermitage Theatre. When in Italy, the architect made detailed measurements of the Vatican loggias, which he used when producing his recreation.

Building work was completed in 1792. The gallery was immediately glazed, as the raw northern made it impossible to leave paintings open to the elements as was the case in the Vatican. (In the nineteenth century the original loggias were also glassed in.) The marble reliefs of the Roman version are reproduced in *grisaille* painting in the Hermitage copy. The apertures in the wall opposite the windows were filled with mirrors, while in the Vatican there are grilled windows giving onto the inner apartments of the palace.

When the New Hermitage was erected in the nineteenth century, the Loggias block was dismantled and reassembled eleven metres to the south. The Classical facade of the gallery which overlooks the small Winter Canal was created to the design of Leo von Klenze (1784–1864), chief architect of the New Hermitage.

The vaults of the gallery contain fifty-two paintings on Old and New Testament subjects, four in each bay. The cycle begins with a depiction of the Creation and ends with the Last Supper. The pictures became known as "Raphael's Bible".

In the decoration of the walls images born of whimsical imagination happily combine with real-life motifs.

The Raphael Loggias
Architect Giacomo Quarenghi, 1783–92

This type of ornament incorporating fantastic elements had appeared back in the Ancient World and Raphael knew it from the ruins of the "Casa d'Oro" — the palace of Emperor Nero that burnt down in A.D. 64 and was accidentally rediscovered during digging work in the 1480s. The ruins that had become buried in the course of time were called grottoes and the artwork found on the remnants of its walls were described as "grotesque". Raphael's own grotesques are striking for the wealth of imagination they betray. The Raphael Loggias are a splendid example of an ensemble that represents a true synthesis of the arts. The architecture of the gallery is founded on human proportions, following the Renaissance idea of Man as "the measure of all things". The calm rhythm of the light, "springy" arches and the noble Classical proportions are an embodiment of the idea of earthly harmony. The impression created by the architect was filled out and enriched by the astonishing fantasy of a brilliant artist.

THE NEW HERMITAGE

Soon after the turn of the nineteenth century, the museum collections which had grown considerably could no longer be comfortably accommodated in the two buildings and in the middle of the century a third building, the New Hermitage designed by the German architect Leo von Klenze, was constructed.

The halls of its upper storey were intended primarily for the stocks of Western European art and accordingly were finished in the traditions of European historical styles.

The main theme in the interior architecture of the Italian Majolica Hall is the use of motifs found in the painted and sculptural decoration of the Renaissance. The ceiling, for example, displays the ornamental caissons (rectangular indentations) common in fifteenth- and sixteenth-century architecture. The frieze that adorns the upper part of the walls features

The Italian Majolica Hall. **Designed by Leo von Klenze, 1851**

The Italian Majolica Hall. **Part of the decoration**

Classical gilded stucco figures of naked boys. The wall paintings use subjects and ornaments popular in the sixteenth century.

On display here is a considerable part of the collection of Italian fifteenth- and sixteenth-century decorative and applied art.

The humanism of the Renaissance period recognised and affirmed the value of earthly existence. This view of the world translated into culture encouraged the flourishing of all types of creativity, including the artistic crafts.

The Ancient World which provided the foundation for the Renaissance was also a source of shapes and motifs for master cabinet-makers: the *cassoni*, wooden marriage chests used to keep a girl's dowry, traced their pedigree back to Ancient sarcophagi and the carving that decorates them often includes Classical figures and grotesque ornament. Also to be found in this hall is an interesting piece of furniture — an archebanc, a bench with arms and a chest beneath the seat.

Masters of other art forms quite often turned their hands to decorative or applied art. Painting served the tapestry industry, artists providing the weavers with cartoons (preliminary full-sized sketches of the design). The Majolica Hall contains a cartoon by Giulio Romano (1492–1546), a pupil of Raphael, that depicts *The Triumph of Scipio Africanus*, the Ancient Roman general who won the war with Hannibal's Carthage.

The most important element in the display, however, the one which gave the hall its name, is a range of items made from majolica — earthenware covered with an opaque tin glaze that was painted before firing.

In the Renaissance majolica production flourished in many Italian cities and towns: Florence, Venice, Derute, Castel Durante, Gubbio (particularly noted for its lustre, an iridescent metallic glaze), Urbino and Faenza (which gave us the name *faience* for such tin-glazed earthenware).

The work of the leading ceramics centres is represented by a wide variety of objects: vases, bowls, jugs, decorative dishes and plates, dishes bearing depictions of young men and women ("wedding dishes" or "lovers' plates") and apothecaries' vessels.

A scudello lid. Majolica. 16th century.
Urbino

Frequently these items are decorated in the spirit of the times with grotesque ornaments, the coats-of-arms of the customer or municipality, scenes from Classical mythology and Christian legend, variations on themes from Ancient works, depictions of Ancient statues and works of architecture, as well as reproductions of the works of Renaissance artists.

Scenes from daily life were also depicted on majolica. The *scudellao*, vessels traditionally presented to new mothers, for example, feature scenes of child-care and child-rearing.

One scene of this kind surrounded by grotesque ornament decorates the plate-shaped lid of the *scudello* produced in an Urbino workshop in the sixteenth century.

The Majolica Hall is home as well to two paintings by Raphael — the *Madonna and Child* or *The Conestabile Madonna* (*ca.* 1504) and the *Holy Family* also known as *Madonna with the Beardless Joseph* (*ca.* 1506).

The Conestabile Madonna is one of the few known youthful works by the great artist, executed while he was still living in his native Urbino. The painting was acquired in Umbria in the nineteenth century from the Marchesi Conestabile, whose name became attached to it.

The pure charm of the Virgin is complemented by the charm of the unprepossessing landscape, still executed with the characteristic fifteenth-century attention to details. The tondo (round) format, beloved of Renaissance artists for its perfect form, sets the compositional rhythm of the soft rounded lines, creating a mood of peace and calm.

The painting is a single whole with the frame carved with grotesques that was probably also designed by Raphael.

Small-sized works such as *The Madonna Conestabile* are a distinctive feature of the early part of Raphael's career.

The *Holy Family*, produced roughly two years later, is not only larger in size, but also executed with the greater degree of generalization that was already characteristic of the High Renaissance.

An adjoining room contains a sculptural work by Michelangelo (1475–1564), the marble *Crouching Boy* which is probably unfinished.

The prototype for this image of a youth squatting with his hands around one foot may have been an Ancient sculpture depicting a boy pulling a splinter

Michelangelo Buonarroti
Crouching Boy. Marble

Raphael (Raffaello Santi or Sanzio)
The Conestabile Madonna. Ca. **1504**

→
The Small Italian Skylight Hall.
Designed by Leo von Klenze, 1851

Michelangelo Merisi da Caravaggio
The Lute Player. Ca. **1595**

out of his foot. The pose gave the master the opportunity to show the tension in the muscles and the manly strength of the beautiful body.

Like their Ancient teachers, the artists of the Renaissance considered physical perfection to be an expression of spiritual beauty. In this work by Michelangelo, however, the calm heroic spirit of the ideal image is disrupted by the motif of spiritual alarm and suffering, physically expressed by the slumped shoulders, the deeply lowered head and the face in shadow. This kind of dramatic intonation is characteristic of the late work by this titan of the Renaissance.

The halls of the New Hermitage were designed with the dimensions of the works in mind. The small "Cabinets" were intended for paintings of no great size.

Three big halls known on account of the way the are lit as the Skylight Halls were created for monumental paintings. The impressive decoration of the ceilings and the decorative ensembles of coloured

stone (contemporary Russian work) are reminders that the museum was conceived as an extension of the main imperial residence.

The Small Italian Skylight Hall contains paintings by the artists of the Bolognese Academy and the followers of Caravaggio as well as Paolo Veronese's monumental work *The Conversion of Saul*. Alongside that hangs a large canvas by one more leading representative of the sixteenth-century Venetian school — Jacopo Tintoretto (1518–1594), *The Nativity of John the Baptist*, the only work by the artist in the Hermitage. The painter depicted the Gospel even as a genre scene in the tradition of the time, but the dynamic arrangement of space, the line and colour scheme create a mood of elevated excitement typical of Tintoretto's expressive manner.

The Cabinet adjoining the Skylight Hall displays the celebrated *Lute Player* (*ca*. 1595), by Michelangelo da Caravaggio (1571–1610), a great innovator in European painting who turned his attention to earthly

Jacopo Tintoretto
The Nativity of John the Baptist. Ca. **1550**

reality. The genre scene is simultaneously an allegory full of both Christian symbols and reminders of the fleeting nature of things. This is one of the first works by the great master in which he used the powerful contrasts of light and shade that came to characterize his work.

The Large Skylight Hall contains work by artists representing various tendencies and schools in Italian eighteenth-century art.

The display includes six immense canvases by the Venetian Giovanni Battista Tiepolo (1696–1770), the last great painter in the Baroque style. Five of them belong to a series produced in the 1720s for the Dolfino family on subjects from Ancient Roman history. The most monumental, *The Triumph of Manius Curtius*, depicts the grand entry into Rome complete with trophy elephants of the military commander who defeated King Pyrrhus of Epirus in 275 B.C.

The dynamic treatment of space, free, expansive manner of painting and elaborate colour effects are elements of the Baroque artistic idiom that established itself early in Tiepolo's career.

A later work by this virtuoso master, *Maecenas Presenting the Liberal Arts to Augustus* (ca. 1745) is on display in one of the cabinets.

In the second half of the eighteenth century the Baroque style gradually waned and popularity passed to those artists who returned to the Classical manner. One of them was Pompeo Batoni (1708–1787), who is represented by several historical, mythological and religious compositions.

Catherine the Great commissioned *Chiron Returning Achilles to His Mother Thetis* (1770). According to the Classical myth, Thetis, a sea nymph, gave her future-hero son to be brought up by the wise centaur.

→
The Large Skylight Hall
Designed by Leo von Klenze, 1851

Pompeo Batoni. *Chiron Returning Achilles to His Mother Thetis.* **1770**

The third (Spanish) Skylight Hall and the neighbouring cabinet house Spanish painting of the fifteenth to seventeenth centuries.

One of the masterpieces of this collection is *The Apostlse Peter and Paul* (late 1580s) by the famous El Greco (1541–1614). The painting presents in striking visual images two different contrasting individuals: the spiritually strong and temperamental Paul and the weak, spiritually meek Peter. The contrast of these two characters stresses the bold courage of Paul and the gentle spontaneity of Peter.

The Hermitage collection of seventeenth-century Spanish paintings is one of the most complete outside the Iberian peninsula (a large number of works by these artists have remained in their homeland). The Skylight Hall presents a whole constellation of masters: Jose Ribera (1591–1652), Francisco de Zurbaran (1598–1664), Bartolomé Esteban Murillo (1617–1682) and Diego Velázquez (1599–1660).

Two paintings provide an introduction to the work of Velázquez, one of the great masters of the "Golden Age" of European painting: *Luncheon* (*ca.* 1617) and *Portrait of the Count-Duke of Olivares* (*ca.* 1640).

Luncheon is among the earliest *bodegones* — a blend of still life with a strong genre element, a field in which the artist was particularly active. A "democratic" theme (common people eating) and verisimilitude in conveying the objects depicted are combined, typically for the art of the time, with Christian symbols: bread and wine — the sacraments, the fish — one of the symbols for Christ, and the red pomegranate seed — the Blood of the Saviour.

Giovanni Battista Tiepolo
The Triumph of Manius Curtius. **1720s**

The Small Spanish Skylight Hall. **Part of the ceiling**

Murillo, an artist highly esteemed in the eighteenth and nineteenth centuries, is represented by a particularly significant quantity of works. He painted both episodes of daily life and religious compositions and quite frequently treated the latter as genre scenes.

In his *Rest on the Flight into Egypt* (1665–70) he creates a lyrical account of an earthly occurrence in a characteristically soft manner.

The Spanish Skylight Hall also houses the only work by Francisco Goya (1746–1828) in the Hermitage collection — his *Portrait of the Actress Antonia Sarate* (*ca.* 1810–11), a gift from the American magnate Armand Hammer in 1972.

One of the most popular rooms in the New Hermitage is the Knights Hall, named on account of the display of Western European armour, cold steel

and firearms from the fifteenth to seventeenth centuries.

Originally the hall was intended for the Tsar's numismatic (coins and medals) collection, a fact reflected in the decor. The painting on the upper part of the walls features round medallions containing the profiles of famous Greeks (Homer, Socrates) and mythical heroes (Ajax, Perseus), similar to those found on medals. Motifs from the Ancient World are the key element in the decoration of the interior.

The collection housed here makes it possible to trace the history of knightly armour from the "Gothic" suits of the fifteenth century to the light armour of the

The Small Spanish Skylight Hall.
Designed by Leo von Klenze, 1851

100

El Greco
The Apostles Peter and Paul. Late 1580s

Bartolomé Esteban Murillo
Rest on the Flight into Egypt. 1665–70

Diego Velázquez
Luncheon. Ca. 1617

103

The knight's armour. **16th century**

sixteenth century and to study the complicated way that sheets of steel were flexibly linked together with hinged joints and straps. The display also includes a child's suit of armour used when teaching a future knight the art of warfare.

In the centre of the room is a memorable mounted parade demonstrating not only body armour, but also horse armour. (For a knight to lose his horse meant he was almost certainly a beaten man.)

By the sixteenth century armour had reached the peak of its development. It provided reliable protection against cold steel, but proved little help against bullets. The spread of firearms forced a reduction in the weight of a knight's equipment and full armour gave way to half-armour which was also worn by infantrymen.

The emergence of reliable firearms meant the end of the road for armour. A last survival was the cuirass

(breastplate and backplate) worn by European heavy cavalry into the eighteenth and nineteenth centuries.

Besides the weapons of mounted warriors, the hall also contains arms used for fighting on foot: two-handed swords, crossbows, pavises (large rectangular shields) and various firearms.

The display demonstrates the practical skill of armourers, but also the superb finish they gave to their creations, the virtuoso technique and artistic taste shown in the chasing, extremely fine engraving, highly elaborate filigree, and effective use of gilding. Exquisitely carved ivory is a feature of many crossbows, harquebuses, muskets and pistols.

The display of Flemish seventeenth-century painting that occupies several halls of the New Hermitage gives us an idea of the work of the greatest masters — Peter Paul Rubens (1577–1640), Anthony van Dyck

The Knights Hall. **Designed by Leo von Klenze**

(1599–1641), Jacob Jordaens (1593–1678) and Frans Snyders (1579–1657) — and a number of other artists from the then Spanish Netherlands. For both scope and artistic standard the Hermitage collection is considered one of the finest in the world.

The canvases represent a broad range of genres including animal painting and the still life. Frans Snyders, one of the greatest exponents of the still life, produced a series of *Shops* in about 1610, while Paul de Vos (*ca*. 1596–1678) one of the most significant painters of animals who specialized in popular scenes of hunting dogs tackling wild beasts, created large decorative *Hunts*.

Works in various genres represent the output of one of the "most Flemish" painters, Jacob Jordaens, the

The Bourguignotte helmet. **1530–40. Italy**
Workshop of Negroli(?)

guardian of the national folklore tradition. Among the artist's favourite subjects was the Feast of the Bean King, held at Epiphany. By long-established custom, the person who discovered a bean in his portion of pie at the festive table became the mock "Bean King".

The Hermitage's *Bean King (ca.* 1638) is one of the finest versions of this composition Jordaens ever produced. The characters of the picture show genuine merriment in raising their glasses and shouting "The King drinks!"

A separate hall is given over to the works of Anthony van Dyck, one of the most brilliant representatives of the Flemish school of painting. Although he worked in a number of genres, van Dyck made his name both at home and abroad first and foremost as a portraitist.

Room of 17th-century Flemish Painting.
Designed by Leo von Klenze, 1851

Invited to London by King Charles I, he spent the rest of his life working in England. The majority of his paintings in the Hermitage collection date from this last period in the artist's career.

The favourite portrait painter of the royal family and the English aristocracy, he produced grand depictions of Charles I, Queen Henrietta Maria and Henry Denvers, the Earl of Denbigh representing the type of formal portrait which van Dyck brought to a peak of perfection that became a standard for European art as a whole. Endowed with subtle psychological insight and the ability to convey the shifts of spiritual and emotional life, even in his large formal portraits the artist created individual characters.

The images of two young sisters depicted in his *Portrait of Elizabeth and Philadelphia Wharton* (second half of the 1630s) is among his most charming and soulful. This work is one of the finest portraits of

Anthony van Dyck
Portrait of Elizabeth and Philadelphia Wharton. **1630s**

children in European art. The splendid palette, with the silvery tonality characteristic of the English period, is an expression of van Dyck's rare colouristic taste and refined painterly manner.

The great Flemish artist's time in Britain played no small part in the emergence in the next century of a brilliant constellation of native English portrait painters.

The Hermitage *Self-Portrait* (late 1620s–early 1630s) is one of the artist's finest depictions of himself. The painting is refined and shows a virtuoso treatment of pearly-grey nuances of tone, while the image is particularly elegant and artistic.

A central position in the collection of Flemish painting is taken by the canvases of "the king of painter

Self-Portrait. **Late 1620s – early 1630s**

and painter of kings" Peter Paul Rubens. Over forty works of different types and genres — portraits, landscapes, narrative compositions, sketches for paintings and monumental frescoes — provide us with an idea of the many-sided work of one of the greatest masters of the European "Golden Age" and one of the greatest artists of the Baroque style.

Rubens's monumental paintings were frequently produced with the help of pupils and assistants who included the finest artists in Flanders. Rubens and his studio often turned out variations on a composition that had proved successful. *The Descent from the Cross* (*ca.* 1618) is a variant of the central part of a triptych painted for an altar in Antwerp Cathedral.

Peter Paul Rubens
The Union of Earth and Water. Ca. **1618**

Peter Paul Rubens
The Descent from the Cross. Ca. **1618**

Peter Paul Rubens. *Roman Charity. Ca*. 1612

The classical precise composition is full of vivid emotional images; the main one — the dead Christ — is both victim and splendid hero.

The Union of Earth and Water (*ca*. 1618) created in the same period is an allegorical work in which Classical gods represent the elements: the Earth by Cybele, the mother of the gods, Water by Neptune, the god of the seas. Their clasped hands are a symbol of the merging of the two elements that give life. This union is the guarantee of the well-being of nature and mankind.

It is possible that this allegory was the artist's response to contemporary events in Flanders. Newly-independent Holland was blockading the mouth of the River Scheldt, denying his homeland access to the sea. Maritime trade was the economic lifeblood of Flanders

and the celebrated artist's painting was a summons to remember the union without which the country could not flourish.

Although he was well acquainted with Ancient art, Rubens did not make his figures resemble marble statues: he created sensual images, embodying male and female principles. The expressive manner of painting conveys the dynamism of life.

A work from the artist's early "Classicist" period is *Roman Charity* (*ca*. 1612), a painting with a strictly geometrical compositional scheme and a powerful plastic quality in the figures. The subject, which was already depicted in Ancient art, is the tale of the young woman Pero who saved her father Cimon, condemned to death by starvation in prison, by feeding him with her breast.

Heroic spirit is a constant element in Rubens's work. He produced a dynamic colour scheme with a abundance of tense and grand red, emotionally elevated images and subjects telling of noble deeds.

Heroic action is the theme of one of the artist's finest creations — *Perseus and Andromeda* (early 1620s). The subject, drawn from Ovid's *Metamorphoses*, is of Perseus saving the Ethiopian princess Andromeda from a sea monster. He wins his victory with the aid of the head of the Gorgon Medusa (the sight of this terrible head with writhing snakes for hair was enough to turn the viewer to stone). Beautiful manliness and no less beautiful femininity are the chief theme of a love song expressed in light, unrestrained painting full of colour reflexes and nuances.

Rubens's most famous paintings also include *Bacchus* (between 1636 and 1640), which the artist produced at the end of his life for his own pleasure and a masterpiece of his portraiture, the *Portrait of a Lady-in-Waiting to the Infanta Isabella* (*ca*. 1625). We can appreciate Rubens's genius as the creator of monumental decorative ensembles from the sketches for the canvases of the *Life of Maria de' Medici* cycle and designs for the decoration of Antwerp for the arrival of a new regent.

Several more halls are occupied by the brilliant collection of Dutch seventeenth-century painting, the beginnings of which date back to Peter the Great. During his stay in Holland the Reformer-Tsar bought paintings to adorn his palaces and some of them subsequently found their way into the Hermitage stocks.

The main part of the collection consists of works by the artists known as "Small Dutch Masters", so-called for the size of their paintings. These canvases are displayed in the Tent-Roofed Hall that gets its name

Peter Paul Rubens. *Perseus and Andromeda.* **Early 1620s**

Tent-Roofed Hall (Room of Dutch Painting). **Designed by Leo von Klenze, 1851**

from its original looking two-pitched ceiling with projecting rafters.

All the fields in which the Small Dutch Masters worked are represented here: the portrait (Kaiser, Hals); the still life (Heda, Kalf, Claesz); the interior (de Witte), animal painting (Potter), landscape (Ruisdael), mythological and biblical subjects (Terbrugghen, Honthorst) and genre painting (Ostade, Steen, Ter Borch).

These are artists who took a sober view of the world around them, and were able to appreciate the value of everyday reality. It was no coincidence that they so happily painted prosaic scenes of the calm, unhurried, even monotonous daily life of their seventeenth-century Holland. But this drowsy atmosphere has a certain attraction: the poetry of a comfortable, well-ordered home, the harmony of a world cultivated and

trimmed by Man for his own well-being. A love of earthly reality gave rise to a distinctive manner of carefully conveying the world of objects, the texture of which was reproduced with tangible verisimilitude. And these painters displayed an equal appreciation of the rich splendour of expensive silver vessels, exotic fruit, precious fabrics and carpets and the humble earthenware and tinplate of a poor home.

This school is superbly represented by one of the greatest of all genre painters Pieter de Hooch (1629–after 1684). In *Mistress and Maid* (*ca.* 1657) he depicts with scrupulous thoroughness a typical Dutch courtyard in which an everyday occurrence acquires significance and a poetic quality. It was in the fairly small rooms of just such houses belonging to the solid burghers that the canvases of the Small Dutch Masters found their place.

A serious attitude to life and the world is at times combined in these paintings with good-natured humour, on occasion crude but never cynical. This is true of the genre scene entitled *The Revellers* by Jan Steen (1626–1679), in which the artist depicts with a merry irony himself and his wife Margaretha.

One of the peaks of European painting as a whole is the work of the great Dutch artist Rembrandt van Rijn (1606–1669). The Hermitage is home to more than twenty of his paintings created at various periods in his life and artistic career.

A product of the artist's youth is *Flora* (1634), a portrait of his wife Saskia in the guise of the Classical goddess of springtime and flowers. The young woman is dressed in a splendid costume of heavy silks created in the painter's imagination and crowned with flowers. Her image looses its everyday character and becomes bathed in a romantic aura. For Rembrandt, who was indifferent to the Classical ideal of beauty, Saskia's unprepossessing looks were an embodiment of feminine charm.

One of the masterpieces by this artistic genius — *Danaë* (1636– *ca*. 1643) —recently suffered a disaster. On 15 June 1985 the painting was splashed with sulphuric acid. For twelve years the experts of the Hermitage easel-painting restoration workshop worked methodically and scrupulously on the precious canvas. *Danaë* went back on display on 14 October 1997.

The subject is taken from Ancient Greek mythology — the tale of a king's daughter who was seduced by Zeus. The all-powerful god visited the beauty in the form of a golden shower.

In Rembrandt's work this appearance is turned into a stream of golden light pouring over the heroine's naked body. An old woman looks out from behind the canopy of the luxurious bed — the servant allotted to the princess in her solitary confinement. Danaë's life and soul have been transformed by the miracle of love.

Rembrandt already displayed an ability to convey the complex world of human emotions in his early paintings; in his celebrated portraits of old men in the

Jan Steen
The Revellers. **1660s**

Pieter de Hooch
Mistress and Maid. Ca. **1657**

Rembrandt Harmensz van Rijn. *Flora.* 1634

118

1650s he produced images the essential idea of which is the inner life transforming the physical shell.

In the famous *Portrait of an Old Man in Red* the great psychologist revealed wisdom, human dignity and nobility. The simple pose and lack of detail give the figure a monumentality, a kind of grandeur. Living light carves out a face with deep wrinkles and the quietly clasped gnarled hands. In some places the paints are laid on thick, in others in a fine layer creating a dynamic texture. The restrained palette of brown and red is infused with vibrant light.

This exceptionally free and absolutely individual manner is especially characteristic of Rembrandt's late work. It is also found in one of his last and most famous masterpieces, the pride of the collection — *The Return of the Prodigal Son* (mid-1660s).

The subject is the Gospel parable of the young man who received his inheritance while his father was still alive but squandered it all away and returned repentant to his father's home. Depicted here is the culminating moment of the story: the meeting between father and son, the act of forgiveness and blessing of the stunned, penitent sinner, the triumph of loving-kindness and goodness.

The Rembrandt hall also contains works by his pupils, artists of his school and his studio (Gelder, Bol,

The Grand Staircase of the New Hermitage. **Designed by Leo von Klenze, 1851**

Victorsz). In the preceding hall are paintings by the great artist's forerunners, his teachers (Lastman, Pynas).

The halls displaying Western European art is anticipated by the Gallery of Ancient Painting. This interior is decorated by wall-paintings on subjects from Classical legends on the origin of the arts and the creations of Ancient artists. They were created by the Munich artist Georg Hiltensperger (1806–1890) who painted on copper using pigments mixed with hot wax in imitation of the Ancient encaustic technique.

Presented here are sculptures of the late eighteenth and early nineteenth centuries, chiefly works by the celebrated Italian Antonio Canova (1757–1822) and the Dane Bertel Thorvaldsen (1770–1824), who was noted in his day.

The most popular of Canova's creations are the sculptural groups *Cupid and Psyche*, *Cupid's Kiss* and *The Three Graces*. His splendid working of the marble and poetic images of figures from Ancient Greek mythology produced a powerful effect on contemporaries. Canova was one of the leaders in his field during the *Empire* period.

The collection of Western European sculpture began to be formed in the Hermitage in the nineteenth century, but even before that large numbers of statues adorned the halls of the palaces. Many of these later came into the museum stocks.

The Grand Staircase of the New Hermitage.
The upper landing

The Twenty-Column Hall. Detal of the ceiling

Gigantomachia. The Crater of Apuliyus. Ca. 350 B.C.
Detal of the painting

Pelica: *The First Swallow. Ca.* 510 B.C.
Greece, Attica. Workshop of Euphronios. Pottery

The Twenty-Column Hall. **Designed by Leo von Klenze, 1851**

Works by eighteenth- and nineteenth-century sculptors can also be found on the upper landing of the magnificent Grand Staircase of the New Hermitage, that leads from the original entrance of Leo von Klenze's building to the halls of the upper floor. Designed in strict Classical style with monumental columns on the upper landing, the staircase forms a single artistic ensemble with the vestibule of the museum.

The halls on the ground floor of the New Hermitage housed the displays of the Ancient Art. Some of the interiors here were created especially for that collection. Von Klenze created the Twenty-Column

Hall, for example, following the traditions of Ancient Greek architecture: two row of Ionic columns divide the hall into three aisles; mighty beams support the coffered ceiling which is painted with palmettes, rosettes and egg-and-dart pattern. Classical motifs are also included in the pattern of the mosaic floor. The walls are decorated with depictions of the gods of Olympus and the heroes of Ancient Greek myths. The hall was intended for the display of ceramic vases (in the nineteenth century it was known as the Hall of Greek and Etruscan Vases), of which the Hermitage has a very rich collection. Still today, alongside other Ancient works of art, visitors can find here vases that

The Jupiter Hall. **Designed by Leo von Klenze, 1851**

on the outskirts of Rome. The work dates from the first century A.D. when the empire was at the height of its power. Its large dimensions (*Jupiter* is about three and a half metres tall), emphatic decorativeness and pretentiousness give us an idea of the tastes of the age when the Colosseum was built and the Arch of Titus erected.

Jupiter was created in the acrolithic technique — of marble and gilded wood; during restoration the latter was replaced by tinted plaster. In his right hand Jupiter holds a depiction of Victoria, the goddess of victory, in his left a sceptre as a symbol of power. Alongside the god is the eagle, the bird sacred to him, a symbol of the sky and sun.

Jupiter. **1st century B.C.**

In compositional terms this *Jupiter* is descended from the famous statue of Zeus created for the temple at Olympia by the Ancient Greek sculptor Phidias (fifth century B.C.). Drawing on Greek originals was a traditional practice for Roman sculptors and it is often thanks to them that we have an idea of works by the great sculptors — Miron, Phidias, Praxiteles and others — that have not come down to us. The Romans collected Greek sculptures, brought them to Rome and used them to decorate their palaces, public buildings and squares.

The Roman works inspired by Greek originals also include the statue of *Athena Campana* (the second part of the name comes from the former owner, the Marchese di Campana whose collection of Ancient works of art was purchased for the Hermitage in Rome

131

The Athena Campana Hall. **Designed by Leo von Klenze, 1851**

in 1861. Like *Jupiter*, this was produced under the influence of a now-lost statue by Phidias. The *Athena Parthenos* was a chryselephantine (gold and ivory) statue created for the Acropolis in Athens. The Roman sculptor made his copy in marble. The goddess is depicted wearing a warrior's helmet and a chiton the long gown of Ancient Greek women, with a cloak falling in heavy folds thrown over it.

The head, evidently already lost in Ancient times, was recreated when the statue was restored in the nineteenth century.

***The Swan Hall.* Designed by Leo von Klenze, 1851**

Quite a number of depictions of the head of Phidias' *Athena* have come down through the ages. In the Special Collection of the Hermitage, for example, there are gold pendants with medallions that bear relief depictions of the head of the *Athena Parthenos*. The pendants were discovered in the Kul-Oba burialmound near Kerch in the eastern Crimea and date from the fourth century B.C.

The museum's extensive stocks also include a range of decorative sculpture used to add interest to gardens, fountains and the inner courtyards of Greek and Roman homes. The architecture of one of the halls in the New Hermitage was designed in imitation of such

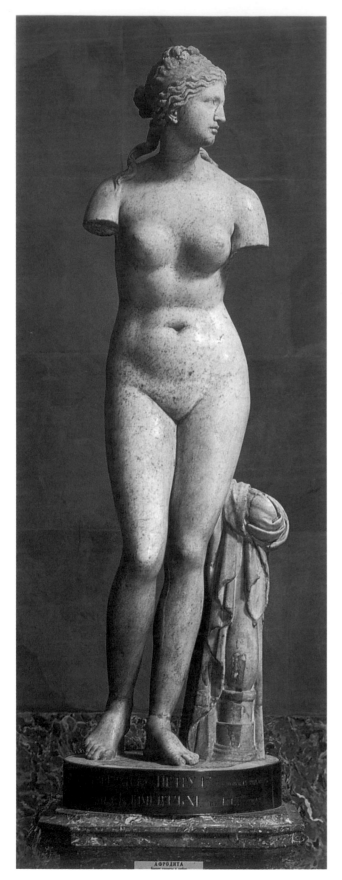

courtyards with a peristyle (colonnade) of white Corinthian columns framing the central space. The hall is used to display part of the collection of decorative sculpture, one of the most prominent themes of which from the Hellenistic period onwards was the depiction of children.

The very first work of Ancient sculpture brought to Russia was probably also created as a garden ornament. This is the statue now known as the *Taurida Aphrodite* (or *Venus*). It was found in the early eighteenth century during excavations in Rome, purchased by Peter the Great and delivered to St Petersburg in 1720. At first *Aphrodite* adorned the Summer Gardens; then, in the 1770s, the Taurida Palace of Prince Grigory Potemkin, hence the present name.

This work too had its older prototype — the *Cnidian Aphrodite* by Praxiteles (fourth century B.C.). As well as features of the art of the Classical period, however, the *Taurida Aphrodite* also gives expression to the aesthetic ideals of the following age, the age of Hellenism: elongated elegant proportions, deliberately exquisite forms and a small head presented with a graceful turn.

The hall in which the statue is displayed is given over to the collection of decorative garden sculpture. Among the most famous works here is a *Dionysus*. It too is a Roman reproduction of a Greek original. The god of fertility and wine is depicted in a temple by an ancient idol of Aphrodite or Kore-Persephone. While the treatment of the face testifies to the influence of Greek sculpture of the fourth century B.C., the overt decorativeness of the clothing falling in whimsical folds is a tribute to the tastes of the Roman era.

The first floor of the New Hermitage is also the location of the Special Collection which contains several thousand artefacts made of precious metals and stones. Among the best known sections of the Special Collection is the stock of "Scythian Gold", pieces of metalwork dating from the seventh to third centuries B.C. The most striking examples of Scythian art (mainly

Aphrodite (*The Taurida Venus*).
2nd century Roman copy of a Greek original (3rd–2nd century B.C.)

The Aphrodite Hall.
Designed by Leo von Klenze, 1851

Snuff-Box. **18th century**

Classical age in jewellery as elsewhere. The chief role in the decoration of snuff-boxes, clocks, and personal ornaments was now played by diamonds.

Snuff-boxes were commissioned particularly often: they were a favourite present and a collector's item. Snuff-boxes were made from gold and silver, decorated with enamel and precious stones. Their lids frequently bore miniature portraits or landscapes.

One of the snuff-boxes kept in the Special Collection has a range of different precious stones (including coloured diamonds). This gem collection in miniature belonged to Empress Catherine the Great.

For the 1900 World's Fair in Paris the celebrated jeweller Carl Fabergé's company produced miniature copies of the Russian imperial regalia: the large and small crowns, the orb and sceptre. Gold, silver, platinum, diamonds (1,328 on the large crown alone), pearls and sapphires were used.

When displayed at the exposition the works brought Fabergé the Gold Medal and the order of the Legion of Honour. Nicholas II acquired the small-scale "regalia" and they have been in the Hermitage since 1901.

In his design for the facades of the New Hermitage von Klenze employed his favourite approach: huge window openings and niches breaking up smooth walls; decorative farming of the windows using sculptural elements and Classical ornaments. In the outside appearance of the New Hermitage he combined features borrowed from Ancient, Renaissance and Baroque architecture.

The facades of the two-storey building are adorned with depictions of Glories alternating with depictions of Genii embodying types of art: drawing, carving, engraving, jewellery. Twenty-eight sculptural images of famous artists, sculptors, engravers and architects were placed in niches and on brackets projecting from the walls. They include Leonardo da Vinci, Titian, Rembrandt and Rubens. The models for these statues, created by Johann von Halbig (1815–1873), were sent to Russia from Munich. They were cast in zinc alloyed with lead and iron at the Krummbügel factory in Moscow.

The main facade of the building, on Millionnaya Street, was embellished by a portico with ten celebrated

Jewellery bouquet. **18th century. By Jérémie Pausier**

Snuff-box. Mineral collection. **18th century**

Copy of the Imperial Regalia. **1900. By Carl Fabergé**

139

Portico of the New Hermitage. **Designed by Leo von Klenze, 1851**

granite Atlantes created by the sculptor Alexander Terebenev (1814/15–1854/59) with the assistance of 150 craftsmen. The sculptor finished each of the faces personally, as well as designing the models from which the whole statues were produced. Von Klenze was very pleased with Terebenev's work, noting their "beauty and noble style". The sculptures were set up in 1848 outside the New Hermitage that was still under construction. It was this grand portico with its gigantic "supporters" that served as the main entrance to the museum in the nineteenth century.

On 7 February 1852 the Hermitage became a public museum and opened its doors to visitors for the first time. It was placed under the auspices of the Ministry of the Imperial Court, in the same way as the theatres. In 1866 the Tsar granted free access to the museum, in other words tickets were no longer required. This step led to an increase in the Hermitage's popularity. The first guides to the museum were published, the first photographs of the Hermitage paintings and the first albums of reproductions (early to mid-1860s). By the beginning of the twentieth century the Hermitage was being visited by some 180,000 people a year.

Figures of Atlantes.
Sculptor Alexander Terebenev, 1851

Auditorium of the Hermitage Theatre

THE HERMITAGE THEATRE

Theatrical performances were one of the favourite diversions of the imperial court in the eighteenth century. The many festivities organized in the residences in and around the capital invariably involved performances featuring Russian and French actors, and sometimes members of the court as well. Special theatres were created in the palaces.

In 1783 on the orders of Catherine the Great, Quarenghi began to construct the Hermitage Theatre alongside the Large Hermitage. The architect himself boasted of the "noble, stern character" of his edifice, which remains one of the finest examples of late-eighteenth-century Russian Classicism. The first performance was given in the theatre as early as 1785, but the building work was only fully completed in 1802.

In designing the auditorium, Quarenghi rejected the traditional tiers of boxes, in favour of an amphitheatre with six concentric rows of benches. In the middle, in front of the stage, armchairs were placed for the Empress and her retinue. The walls and columns were faced with artificial marble in a variety of warm tones. The capitals of the columns bore depictions of theatrical masks. The decoration of the amphitheatre also featured statues of the god Apollo and the nine muses, and medallions with relief depictions of composers, poets and dramatists, including Molière, Racine, Voltaire and the Russian Alexander Sumarokov. The statues and medallions were the work of the sculptor Concesio Albani (died 1818). The benches of the amphitheatre and the floor were covered with coloured cloth. Ten chandelier-like candelabra were made to light the auditorium. The stage was considerably larger than the seating area and was flanked with dressing-rooms. There were also mechanisms for changing the scenery and producing various theatrical effects.

142

Auditorium of the Hermitage Theatre. **Architect Giacomo Quarenghi, 1783–89**

In the course of the nineteenth century building work was carried out in the theatre several times, altering its original appearance. In the 1890s, under the direction of the architect Alexander Krasovsky the ceilings of the building were replaced and the finish of the walls and columns renewed. At that time the great crystal chandelier with electric lights was installed, together with machinery for raising and lowering scenery. In the decoration of the auditorium, however, Krasovsky strove to follow Quarenghi's original intentions and remove the distortions that had appeared in the interim. The Hermitage Theatre has seen notable performances by some of the great names of the Russian stage, including the celebrated singers Yelizaveta Sandunova (1772/77–1826) and Fiodor Chaliapin (1873–1938). In recent years this, the oldest theatre building in St Petersburg has again become the venue for ballet and opera productions, as well as concerts by chamber and symphony orchestras.

Five outstanding works of architecture constructed in the course of the eighteenth and nineteenth centuries — the Winter Palace, Small, Old and New Hermitages, plus the Hermitage Theatre — combined with extremely rich collections put together over centuries make up that unique phenomenon in Russian and world culture that is known around the globe simply as the Hermitage.

Эрмитаж

Альбом (на английском языке)

Издательство «Альфа-Колор»
Санкт-Петербург
Тел./Факс (812) 326-8384
E-mail: alfac@mail.wplus.net